The Why of Me

Diane Marie Schiltz

PublishAmerica
Baltimore

ISBN: 1-4241-2297-X
PUBLISHED BY PUBLISHAMERICA, LLLP
www.publishamerica.com
Baltimore

Printed in the United States of America

Acknowledgment

I am grateful to Mary, who initiated the idea of my writing a book. My daughter Anne Marie gave me continual encouragement as I would send her each chapter. My daughter Kari gave me a computer and my friend Louise gave me a printer. These gifts enabled me to write the book. I am totally grateful to Louise, who helped me in the later stages getting the book to the publisher. Without your help, Louise, this book never would have been published. Thank you all for your undying support and encouragement.

Foreword

Kari—*The Why of Me* is a very honest book about living with mental illness. My mother shares in detail different facets of her life as a mentally ill person. It is especially inspirational to know that after all she has battled with, she now leads a very normal and happy life, spending a majority of her time helping her daughters with her grandchildren.

Barbara—What struck me when I read Mom's book is how she must have felt through the years. Mental illness, unlike a physical illness, is so hard for people to accept or understand. As a child, I believe I was in denial about Mom's illness and that was my way of coping. As a teen, I was embarrassed about her behavior and her time spent away from home. Now, as an adult, I know much more about what was going on, and am more compassionate and supportive.

Anne Marie—As I grew older, I realized that the many times "Mom had to go away because she was sick," it was not just the basic flu. Reading this book opened my eyes to what a strong dad we had. Many times he had to raise us, provide for us and protect and love us when Mom was out of the picture. I truly believe that I have the very best mom and dad in the world.

Contents

The Why of Me

"He who has a why to live for can bear almost any how." Nietzsche

Introduction

For a long time now, I have had the idea that I would like to somehow pay back the mental health system for all the help I have received over the years. About ten years ago, I made an attempt to write a book. That book has been sitting on a shelf for all these years. Just recently a friend of mine said to me, "You have a book sitting on the shelf which you have never tried to publish?" After talking with her, I was moved to take the book down off the shelf and look at it. I was surprised at what I saw. Even though I was very ill while I was writing it, the book itself had no value. However, some of the stories in the book simply needed to be told, as they described my life as a mental patient.

While studying this book and trying to glean something of interest, it came to me that I had stored away many writings. Once I began searching through my folders, I came across not one but many stories of my past which I had written while in the throes of mental illness. When I had thoroughly perused all of my writings, I came up with a skeleton book. I made the decision to try once again to write a book about my mental illness, only now I had better motivation for writing it, since I was well. I could write not only about my illness, but about my wellness. My longtime dream to help pay back the mental health system began to take form. If I wrote a book now, I could conclude it with a happy ending. People who read my book could be inspired to think that there may be a rainbow at the end of the storm.

As my new book began to take shape, I often thought about the possibility that my writing could become an inspiration to the many sufferers of mental illness. They could be led to see that there is a way out of the maze of suffering. Perhaps because of my refusal to be a victim of my illness, I managed to find my own way out. Perhaps I was healed through the help of many fine doctors. Perhaps my deep spirituality gave me the courage to stop at nothing short of success in my life.

Whatever the answer may be, I have found my way out of the maze. I wish to communicate in the best way I know how, where I was yesterday and where I find myself today. If I can achieve this by telling my story, then I will have found my answer as to how to help others. This is the very basic reason I have for attempting to write about my life as a mental patient. I have given fictitious names to all of the doctors and hospitals.

CALEDONIA, Minnesota

"I began to have an idea of my life, not as the slow shaping of achievement to fit my preconceived purposes, but as the gradual discovery and growth of a purpose which I did not know." Johanna Field

I had a beautiful childhood. My parents showered us children with much love and caring. My father, who worked in a bank his entire life, provided modestly for his family. I was born between two boys, one and a half years younger and one and a half years older. Six years later, a little sister was born, and nine years later, another sister. We received another surprise when my youngest sister was born when I was twenty-one. I always considered myself fortunate to have two brothers to play with. They were rough and tough and so was I. In fact, I was the epitome of a tomboy, liking nothing better than to play football, cops and robbers, cowboys and Indians, and to engage in snowball fights on the skating rink. I could play the roughest games with the roughest boys, and I loved it. But I was also this demure little girl who loved to play with my dolls. In our yard there was an island of lilac bushes interspersed with lily of the valley flowers; it was a virtual paradise. In the middle of these bushes was enough space for me to play house by myself for hours.

We had a huge yard with several good climbing trees. I loved to climb the butternut trees, the apple trees and the poplar trees. I became an expert trapeze artist, jumping from branch to branch, hanging by my legs and sitting on the topmost branch looking out over the world as though I were on a ship atop the highest sails. I climbed trees even when I was considered too old to climb trees. Nothing could keep me from this my favorite past-time, not even age.

When I was about 10 years old, my mother went to work. She knew that we children were old enough to take care of ourselves. She would have a heart attack if she knew some of the mischief we got into. There was a big "haunted" house a few blocks away and I had always fantasized about exploring it. One day, I was able to coax my brothers into entering this house. It was a wonderful adventure measuring up to my wildest dreams. We were never caught, but I dread to think what would have happened to us if we had been.

My brothers had friends, and these boys thought up enough mischief for all of us. I remember going to town and climbing onto the tops of buildings and jumping from roof to roof. I was the only girl but found no trouble in keeping pace with all the boys.

Running away from home did not seem like a terrible a thing to do. One afternoon, my brothers were fighting so fiercely that I threatened to run away if they did not stop. They didn't stop, so I set out walking along the railroad tracks. After going a long way, my brother Eddie came up behind me and said, "If you don't come home, I'm going to break your arm." I said, "Go ahead and break it." He returned home dejectedly without me.

I walked carelessly down the tracks until I suddenly stopped. A big black and white cow was standing in the middle of the tracks just ahead of me. If there was one thing I was afraid of, it was cows. Being very cautious, I changed direction and started walking across the fields. After walking for about ½ hour, I saw the highway in the distance and decided to walk along it instead. Before too long, I heard a car pull up behind me. It was my mother! By that time, I was greatly relieved to see her.

I missed having my mother around to keep the boys under control.

I thought that perhaps my running away would convince her to quit her job, but it didn't. I had to do a lot of housework to help her out, and I resented this. While I worked, the boys played, and I didn't think this was fair.

While growing up, we were encouraged to play musical instruments. My brother Eddie and I both played the clarinet and my brother Larry played the trumpet. When it came time for me to join senior band with the clarinet, I had to give it up because there was just one clarinet between Eddie and me and we were both in senior band. My parents told me to switch to drums, which I hated. Because I stopped taking drum lessons without consulting my parents, I was punished severely. I was forbidden to go to any of the basketball games for an entire year.

My parents had the reputation of being the strictest parents in town. All of my friends had a healthy fear of them. I thought we all ended up being well-behaved children despite this strict discipline, even though we had our difficult times.

I consider myself fortunate to have had such a wonderful childhood with so much time for creative play and so many good times with my brothers and younger sister. But there was always a cloud over my head. My parents fought often. Their fighting could get pretty fierce at times, although I never saw my father use physical force. Both my mother and father had a terrible temper. My mother would resort to throwing things, like dishes, across the room. We cowered out of sight during these storms. Their fighting often left us in tears. Many times, I felt as though I was the cause of the fights.

My mother loved to dress me like a little doll. She would beg for money from my dad so that she could buy beautiful clothes for me. This happened especially at Easter time. We always looked our very best on Easter at Mass. Because Easter was preceded with so much fighting, I can't say I enjoyed parading around in my Easter finery. Instead, I felt that it was my fault that they argued so much about the money being spent on my Easter outfit.

All of us children were very healthy, until I was 10 years old. At this time I had a rare illness—a combination of rheumatic fever and chorea. The best way to describe chorea is that it was like a child having a nervous breakdown. I had to take very expensive medication and had to rest a lot. At the slightest provocation, I would throw myself on the bed and cry for a prolonged period of time. I became paranoid and was afraid of certain children at school, especially boys. For a long time I had to stay home from school and rest. My mother encouraged me to get well by promising that when I was better I could join art class. This was something great to look forward to, as I considered myself a budding artist.

This illness made me feel very self-conscious, for I experienced severe tremors, involuntary movements of my arms and I couldn't walk straight. I felt that my parents were ashamed of me whenever I was in public with them. For myself, I couldn't understand what was happening to my body and my mind. It was a very frightening illness. Because of the rheumatic fever side of the illness, my body ached and I had to be rubbed down with ointment every night. I always had the feeling that my mother was afraid of my illness—afraid of me. The smallest thing would set me off. Eventually, the rest and the medication worked and I became well again.

My parents always instilled in us a need for perfection in whatever we did. We were expected to have good grades in school. If we came home with bad report cards, we were punished. If we came home with good reports, we were rewarded. Eddie and I found school to be very interesting and challenging. We loved to excel. Larry, on the other hand, wasn't too keen about school. He was the class clown throughout his years of grade school and high school. Even though we came from a middle-class family we were all able to attend college because of the loans our father made to us. We were each expected to pay back our loans. This proved a great incentive for all of us. The fact that our parents so valued our education was a great asset in our lives.

Spirituality also played a big part in our lives. We all attended a Catholic grade school and a Catholic high school and were encouraged to go to daily Mass while attending these schools. My father especially encouraged us to attend Sunday Mass. Easter and

Christmas were occasions of much celebration because it was a spiritual experience for each of us starting at a very young age. We often prayed the rosary as a family. Again, my father was instrumental in getting the family to gather around for this spiritual devotion.

I believe that because of my rich spiritual upbringing, I have been influenced in my life to a great degree towards living a deeply spiritual life. I believe I have my father to thank for this.

Because my parents fought so often during my childhood, I vowed that when I got married and had children of my own, I would never fight with my husband. I kept this vow. Most of our 20 years of marriage, we never fought. Towards the end, however, we did fight many times.

I am sure that this is why the marriage failed. Of course, in the twenty year span of our marriage, differences arose. Because I was so fearful of expressing my opinion, I lived a very frustrating existence. I paid a very great price for this "peace". As a child, there were times when I begged my parents to get a divorce. In the end, they were able to iron things out. I believe their marriage went a lot smoother by the time my two youngest sisters came along. During my own marriage, my mental illness continued to get worse and worse.

It is impossible to say why I was mentally ill. It could have been for many reasons. I have always been told that my mental illness was caused by a chemical imbalance and that is why my brain malfunctioned. I will probably never know the truth. I am immensely grateful that my own daughters never experienced this illness. Perhaps by maintaining a peaceful household, I was able to give them the peace of mind that I never had as a child.

As a student at Loretto Catholic High School, I was very busy. Actually "busy" wasn't the word. I was extremely involved. For the last three years of high school I was a part of the Triple-Trio singing at many school gatherings and even on TV. I took piano lessons all throughout high school and was editor of the yearbook. During my junior and senior years, I worked for the Clerk of Court. I took all college prep classes and was named Salutatorian of my high school graduating class.

We heard a lot about religious vocations from the nuns at Loretto. Perhaps I was very vulnerable to the influence of the nuns because I became intrigued with the thought of becoming one. Because I was very shy, and never dated boys at all, my pastor discouraged me from going into the convent right out of high school. Every night, my friend Laurie and I would meet and stand under the lamp post discussing our future. We both felt called to be a nun, but Laurie was not very happy with the idea. She thought that God was calling her, but she didn't want to go into the convent. I, on the other hand, thought of it as tempting—something to be considered.

Perhaps the reason Laurie didn't like the idea was because she had a boyfriend. I never dated so I had no idea what the attraction to the other sex was like, even though I had often had "crushes" on boys. Actually, I was in the midst of an anguished conflict at this time in my life, feeling that God wanted me to be a nun, but not totally happy with this idea either. It was at this troubled time in my life that I went for a long ride with my two best friends, Laurie and Sharon.

Even though my parents had forbidden me to ride with any of my friends outside of town, Laurie and Sharon convinced me to go with them for a ride. We drove to LaCrescent and were on our way to Brownsville. As we were driving along the river, with a railroad track on one side of the highway next to the river and hills on the opposite side, I was taken aback by the beauty of the scene. I asked Laurie if we could get out and watch the sun go down as it was beginning to set with brilliant color. Laurie and Sharon both laughed at me, but I insisted. Finally, Laurie said that she would let me out but that they would keep on driving. So Laurie stopped the car, I got out and she took off. I tried to jump on the back of the car, which was very foolish. Pretty soon they were out of sight. I stayed there by myself, knowing that they would turn around and pick me up.

Soon after, the sun set and darkness settled in. There was no sign of Laurie and Sharon. I walked along and cars started slowing down, but I was afraid someone would stop to pick me up so I decided to walk among the weeds down by the railroad tracks so people wouldn't see me. This was most likely why Laurie and Sharon couldn't find me when they turned around and came back looking for me. They finally gave up looking for me and drove back to Caledonia, where Laurie called my mother. When she asked my mother if I was there, my mother noted something strange in Laurie's voice and demanded, "Laurie, tell me what happened!" So Laurie had to tell her what happened to me, that they couldn't find me. Immediately, my mother and father went out looking for me. They went everywhere, even onto the houseboats along the river.

As I was walking along and it was getting very dark, I discovered a sign that said the next town was five miles away. I decided that I should walk toward that town as I had no idea how far the town behind me would be. So I kept on walking and it got darker and darker. I was frightened by every animal noise I heard up in the hills. By the time I finally arrived in Brownsville my legs were shaking so badly I could hardly stand up. I didn't know what to do. I thought I would go to a nearby house and ask to use the phone. As I started walking toward the house, about five or six dogs came running out from nowhere and started chasing me. They were all barking loudly. I had always been warned about farm dogs by my dad so I started running away from them. I saw that I was closer to the garage than to the house, so I ran into the garage and jumped on top of the car. I was out of reach of the dogs but I felt trapped because every time I started to get down they started barking again. I stayed in that position for a long time when I started thinking, "How am I going to get out of here?" I felt for the window of the car and realized that it was open a crack. I reached around in the dark and found a tool on the roof of the garage. I used this tool to pry the window open and then unlocked the door and climbed into the car. I quickly locked the door. I realized that I was safe from the dogs, but I wasn't sure what I should do now that I'm in the car. I decided to start honking the horn and turning the lights on. I kept honking and honking. I had no idea what time it was but figured that it was late and everyone was probably in bed.

Finally a mean and grumpy man came out of the house and down to the garage. He couldn't imagine what anyone was doing in his car. He ordered me to get out, but he was so mean that I was afraid to leave the car. I told him that I wouldn't get out until he brought his wife down. So he went back and got his wife. Both were in their pajamas when they came back. I told them my predicament but he just kept demanding that I get out of his car. I asked them if they would let me use their phone. He said they didn't have a phone so I asked him if he knew of someone who did and he said no one in town had one. Finally, he told me that the tavern down on the river bank had a phone, so he gave me a flashlight and directed me down to the river.

I walked down to the riverside where they directed me, and there was a big tavern. Of course it was closed at that time but I could tell there were living quarters on top of the tavern, so I just stood there and yelled as loud as I could, "I'm lost, can someone please help me?" Finally, a man and woman came out and I told them about how I was lost and asked if I could use their phone. They let me use it so I called home. My mother answered and immediately started to cry. Before long, she drove up with her friend and took me home. It was 3 a.m. when I finally reunited with my family. That night I cried in bed for hours, realizing how I had frightened my parents.

After this incident, my parents forbade me to be friends with Laurie and Sharon. I spent all of my free time with my new friend, Beth. Before too long my parents decided that since I seemed to be on the verge of delinquency, they would send me to Florida with my grandmother and that maybe that would take care of the problem. While there, I went by bus to the beach each day. It wasn't long before I met a very cute boy by the name of Michael and we spent all of our time together. One day I decided to rent a raft to go out on the ocean alone. After a long time out by myself, I was suddenly awakened by a man who had swum out after me. He asked me, "Do you realize how far out you are?" I could hardly see the beach, I was out so far. If he hadn't come out after me, I might have drifted out into the ocean far away from the shore. I believed then and I believe now that my guardian angel was watching out for me.

When it was time to go back to Minnesota and I had to say goodbye to my friend Michael, I felt a strong tug at my heart. This was my first boyfriend ever, and I was on my way back to Minnesota to enter the convent.

By now my parents had more or less forgotten the incident of the tavern and allowed me once again to be friends with Laurie and Sharon. One night we went to the circus together, and while there I met a man by the name of Ken. He was six years older than I was. We dated right up until the time I left for the convent. Later on, I was to discover that while I was in the convent he wrote several love letters to me which I was never told about. One day, I was able to go back to visit my parent's house as my grandparents were celebrating their 50th wedding anniversary. My mother arranged for Ken to meet me at her home. It was at this time that he told me about the love letters he had sent to me. Even after meeting with him, I had no trouble going back to the convent, for I had fallen in love with God. Nothing else mattered to me anymore. At least I now felt that I met the criteria for being convent material, because I had dated two young men.

WINONA, Minnesota

"Destiny is not a matter of chance, it is a matter of choice; it is not a thing to be waited for; it is a thing to be achieved." William Jennings Bryan

Upon entering the convent, I was given a battery of psychological tests. Our convent was connected to the College of St. Teresa, so we were tested along with all the other college freshmen. Even though I took the test purposely trying to reveal my unstable condition, I was accepted, presumably without any psychological problems.

I was called a postulant this first year. We postulants lived in a big house on campus. Sister Michaea was our postulant mistress. She was a lovely woman with deep, dark blue, meaningful eyes, which were in sharp contrast to her pale complexion. She disciplined us with merely a look. I had never before met a woman so beautiful and motherly, with such high ideals, who was so at peace with herself and her chosen way of life. She took great care of the souls entrusted to her by nurturing the spiritual growth of each and every young woman, and we, in turn, grew to love her deeply.

I put Sister Michaea on a pedestal and to this day I feel she still belongs there. She was one person in my life who lived up to the ideals I held for her. All along, I was very enthused about my vocation and was completely happy and fulfilled. The convent was where I would stay.

After a year of postulancy, we were to go to the Novitiate. This was in a huge, beautiful convent called Assisi Heights, in Rochester, Minn. It was set high on a hill overlooking the city. This building also housed all the old and feeble nuns.

ROCHESTER, Minnesota

"Joy is the serious business of heaven." C.S. Lewis

Finally, we were ready for the Novitiate, which is another word for the cloister. Family and friends were allowed to visit only once a month. Other than that we were completely shut off from the outside world. We would eat, drink, sleep, pray and play within these walls until the time of our profession, when we took our vows.

My conception of this time in my life was that it was comparable to heaven. Of course, we had to work very hard, but I enjoyed the various types of jobs that I was assigned to. I especially enjoyed living with a group of young women who had devoted their lives to serving God. I was amazed at these fine young women who had given their lives to God at the prime of their life.

We were told to expect a "honeymoon" feeling while in the Novitiate. Extra graces were given to us to help us through the hard times. I felt as though I had been granted much help and strength from God because everything came easy to me. It was easy for me to keep silence. It was very easy to meditate at 6 a.m., which was not true for most of the novices. I loved saying the daily Office and especially loved the dark little chapel where we said our night prayers together and where we could remain for our own private devotions if we so wished.

Near our bedrooms on the second floor was a large balcony where many of the nuns would go after night prayer to watch the sun set on the close of a prayerful and peaceful day. There was something very special about seeing these young women in their night robes, drinking in the surrounding beauty while talking with their God.

Not all of the novices found it as easy as I did. Most of the girls hardly kept silence at all. I don't think we were expected to keep it. Some of the novices fell asleep on and off during morning meditation. There were times when the novices would giggle during night prayer, myself included, but I was usually more serious about everything than I should have been.

I did my work cheerfully and well and got along with whoever was in charge of me for different types of work. The novices spoke of certain jobs with fear and dislike. One such assignment was kitchen and bakery duty, under the supervision of Sister Josette, who was supposed to be a hard taskmaster, one who demanded perfection. Eventually, I was assigned to a job under her supervision. I admired her with a healthy and fearful attitude. I imagine she knew how I respected her and often thought I observed just a trace of a smile beneath that severe mask of her face.

My job was to help see that all the old sisters received and ate their food. I would wheel them from their rooms; pin on their napkins and help spoon feed some of them. I couldn't believe how old and stubborn some of them were, while others were so young at heart and pleasant to be with.

At the time I was working in the infirmary, one of the oldest nuns was dying. I could hear her crying in pain as I cleaned the dining area, which was right next door to her room. A couple of times I went in to visit her and was told she was experiencing the "death rattle". I had never seen anyone close to dying, and my reaction was one of revulsion. She had the "death rattle" for about 10 days. She was nothing but a bundle of bones and her face looked like a skeleton.

I couldn't imagine anyone wanting to live in that condition. She didn't want to die and was fighting it to the last, but finally she died. I realized this when I saw Father Glen come out of her room. I cried and was possessed with such a feeling of fear and mystery that cannot be described. I quickly ran from the dining room down into the novitiate kitchen to share my first confrontation with death.

Shortly after this another nun died, and we were told to keep a vigil throughout the day and night. I was one of the "lucky" ones who had to go at night. We were sent in two's. My partner and I went between 2 a.m. and 3 a.m. We walked through the dark, long corridors, shaking with fear and jumping at every little noise. We had to go into the poorly lit chapel where the nun was laid out, and we knelt right up beside the coffin where we prayed for an hour. I somehow managed to get through this vigil which was my first and my last.

Even though I tried to be a good novice most of the time, there were times when my mischievous nature came to the foreground. On April Fool's Day, I asked Sister Cashel to help me play a joke. We went behind the sacristy to look for a way of ringing the church bells. I saw a button and when I pushed it to "on" the bells in the tower started ringing loudly. We ran out of church because we were frightened. We listened to the bells ring for about ten minutes and realized that no one was turning them off, so we knew we had to run back and turn them off ourselves.

That evening everyone was talking about it. Sister Lucretia, our novice mistress, said that they had received many calls from people in Rochester who heard the bells and wondered who had died. She said that this was a very grievous action and she wanted the person or persons who did it to confess. So Sister Cashel and I decided we would have to tell them that we were the ones who did it. When we told them, there was quite a big ruckus because no one could believe these sweet, innocent novices would ever do anything so horrible. We were punished by having to confess it and being recognized as the rascals who did it. No one who knew us thought we had anything like that in us. They thought we were little angels, and up to that point, I guess we had been. Since I was the instigator, I received the greater punishment. We were both very fearful that we would be kicked out of the convent. I made a special trip to visit the Grotto, a beautiful shelter made of stone with a statue of Mary inside. This was at the bottom of the hill leading to the convent. There, surrounded by luscious trees and beautiful flowers, I prayed earnestly that I would be allowed to stay.

Another time I got in trouble was when I found some roller skates in the basement and another novice and I decided to use them. We had the best time in the world, but little did we know the sounds in the tunnel resounded very loudly in the dining room up above. We were harshly disciplined for our "fun". Most of the time I was very serious about being a good novice.

There were times, I'm sure, when the other novices must have looked at me and thought "holier than thou". I was honeymooning with God. I chose to keep general silence stricter than anyone else. I did my work with painstaking perfection. I loved to go into the chapel and pray whenever there was free time. I counted my faults as numerous and confessed them with much sorrow and contrition. Finally, I came to the point where nothing meant more to me than pleasing God and being in His favor. I wanted to become a Contemplative. A Contemplative Order is one where the nuns pray continuously. They don't perform functions such as nurses or teachers, as an Active Order does. They pray from morning to night.

I made this wish known to my novice mistress and she was quite distressed. She made an appointment with me during which I should tell her more about this idea. She mentioned that eight other novices were pursuing this same thought. She told me she was sure it was the devil's doing, to coax us to give up our position in the Active Order and then to leave us without any religious life at all. She was sure that if we left we would never make it into another form of religious life.

I battled with this interpretation every night for about two weeks. I became more and more upset over the prospect that this might be a temptation rather than a blessing. I couldn't understand how something seen as good by me should seem so disastrous to my novice mistress. We were like seeds in a hothouse. Our lives were so immersed in God's presence and favor we simply couldn't help but be drawn more closely to the One we loved. Or was it so simple? Was the devil actually behind it all? It was very puzzling.

I began to grow quite nervous. My arms and legs ached. I was assigned dish room duty and was appointed as supervisor of the dish room. This was supposed to be the toughest of all assignments. I threw myself into it with every fiber of my being and achieved success as a supervisor. We finished the dishes on time every night and polished the room from top to bottom on Saturdays. This was a great achievement. It left me little time to think, which was the objective Sister Lucretia had in mind. Only now I began to tire easier and to a greater degree. I couldn't concentrate on my lessons, I began to be possessed by the idea of perfection, my confessions were ridden with scrupulosity, my prayers at the Way of the Cross were more pleading and meaningful, and I wanted to suffer for Christ in whichever means He chose to give me. I was prepared to do anything for Christ, even the most unmentionable thing, which would be to have my vocation taken away.

One night I read the story "Mr. Blue", a true story of a modern day contemplative. As I walked up the stairs I stopped at the landing where the statue of the Blessed Virgin Mary stood. I thought I saw tears falling down her face, so I touched them and tasted them. They were salty, just like real tears would be. I was certain this had some meaning for me. I was to do something that made even the Blessed Virgin cry. Suddenly, it all came to an end. At the age of 20, after two and a half years in the convent, horrible things were happening to me. My entire body ached. I started isolating myself from the other novices. More conscious of sin than ever before, I started recording my sins. When going to confession, which was once a week, I had to ask the Priest to turn the light on in the confessional so I could read my list. All of my free time was spent in church, adoring the Eucharist. I was so pious that I was extremely cautious about keeping general silence which meant I never talked with the other novices. The conceit and pride of my new way of life gave way to alarm. I was no longer at peace with myself or my God.

After the experience of seeing the Blessed Virgin cry, which I realize was not real; I began to go downhill rapidly. One day after work I was so exhausted that I sat down in the first chair I saw. This was isolated from the rest of the novices and as it was recreation time, I suppose it seemed odd that I would choose to sit quietly by myself. Sister Lucretia noticed me and walked over to where I was sitting. She asked me why I was choosing to be so unsociable, if I was sitting there feeling sorry for myself. When I told her how tired and achy I was, she told me she would make a doctor appointment for me. I had no idea that the doctor she was referring to would turn out to be a psychiatrist. Early one morning I dressed in my outdoor garb, put on my gloves and cheerfully walked out of the convent with Sister Lucretia. On the way, she told me I was going to see a psychiatrist. That puzzled me and made me very anxious. I couldn't understand the reason behind it because the pain I was experiencing was very real and very physical.

At this hospital most of the nurses were nuns from our Order. The psychiatrist was a Franciscan nun. I went in and talked with her for no longer than one hour. During this time, I cried almost steadily. It seemed that every question she asked pertained to my life before entering rather than to my life in the convent. At the end of the hour she talked with Sister Lucretia.

On the way back to the convent, Sister Lucretia told me that I was to leave the convent and that I should never again try to enter the religious life. I couldn't believe it! This wasn't what I wanted and I was totally unprepared for such a shock. I cried uncontrollably, yet I knew tears wouldn't help. Sister Lucretia took me to the chapel to let me cry and pray. I felt utterly dejected at being rejected by God. I accepted this as the will of God and never again did I try to enter the convent, even though I often yearned to do just that. After my visit, she took me down to see Sister Josette of whom I had become quite fond. On the way, Sister Lucretia told me that Sister Josette had cancer and would probably not live very much longer. I couldn't imagine that anyone as tough and great as she would ever die so young. I guess it made my trial a little easier to bear. We cried and said goodbye to each other.

The novices had been practicing for the Christmas program with great intensity. It was to be a fantastic program.

I was forbidden to tell any of the other novices about my leaving. Because of this, I felt very much alone and isolated. While I was still among them I would look at one or the other and muse on the fact that I would probably never see them again. This left me anguished and deeply disturbed. Finally, I became too exhausted to go to choir practice. I couldn't even walk down the hall. I was sent to the infirmary where I was to remain until the day after Christmas at which time I'd leave for home.

I was in the infirmary for about three weeks. The time went slowly and painfully. I decided to utilize this time by saying my farewells to the many nuns I had worked with. I wrote notes to each of them that would be sent after my departure. I couldn't write to my fellow novices, however. I know that these good-byes were said with much emotion. Yet I accepted the prospect of leaving much better than I would have expected. It amazed me when Sister Lucretia asked me if I was thinking about suicide. At that early time in my illness the thought of suicide was very foreign to me. Deep depression had not yet pervaded my being as it would do in the coming months and years. This occurrence was merely a hint of what I would undergo in the future.

One of the most tormenting memories comes to me every Christmas. This is because of the Christmas program. A Christmas program in Assisi Heights' Motherhouse, under the direction of Sister Bernardine, is a very different thing from any other Christmas program. She is truly a great musician. Her idea of a chorus singing was that every individual must sing exactly on key, must breathe with the rest, must pronounce with precision and must be perfect. It was such a joy to listen to her choirs, much less take part in them. Practices were exhausting, for what she expected was indeed perfection. Yet I'm sure that anyone hearing the final product felt it was worth all the effort.

I was allowed to sing in the Christmas program with the rest of the novices. For this I was extremely grateful. Every song we sang that night had a special meaning for me. When we started to sing "The Little Drummer Boy," I couldn't sing, as I was all choked up and tears were flowing down my face. It seemed as though the words were directed right at me. I was the little boy who had no gift good enough for Him. I played my drum the best I could for Him and was sure that God was as pleased with my effort as He was pleased with the gift of the drummer boy. For at least 10 years afterward, Christmas was an emotional struggle for me, as I was always reminded by Christmas music of this sad, hard time in my life.

Christmas Day finally came. I begged to go along with the rest of the novices as they walked to the hospital to sing carols through the halls. I was told that the trip would be too hard for me, but that I could assist Father Glen at Christmas Mass. This was a great honor. I didn't do too great of a job, however, as I was preoccupied even during the Mass and missed ringing the bell a couple of times.

The following day, Sister Lucretia brought out my black suitcase and an outfit of street clothes. I couldn't believe how skinny I looked with something on other than my long white habit. I weighed about 100 lbs. I certainly was way too thin.

The sisters had called my parents and asked them to come and take me home. I kissed Sister Lucretia and Mother Callista goodbye. On the way home I felt very strange. I couldn't believe how loudly my mother and father talked. I learned later that whenever I was extremely nervous I couldn't tolerate noise because noises were amplified in my ears at least 10 times. Another surprise was to await me as I entered my parent's home. I had never thought we lived in a small house, but after being used to the convent with its' long corridors and spacious rooms, I felt as though I were walking into a dollhouse, it seemed so small.

I was a stranger in my own home for a long time. I didn't know what to do with myself. I did some painting, but nothing really interested me. I laid on my bed a good deal of the time, drowning in deep despair. I was suffering from neurasthenia and the whole world looked dark and forbidding.

Eventually I began working on oil painting in earnest. Some of my best work was done at this time because I was so withdrawn I could concentrate entirely on my painting. I focused on what I was doing and forgot about everything else. My life was pretty much at a complete standstill.

LA CROSSE, Wisconsin

"The human spirit is never finished when it is defeated...it is finished when it surrenders." Ben Stein

Finally, my older brother Eddie, with whom I had always been very close, came home for a visit. He talked me into finishing my college education. It was mid-semester time, so I decided to take exams for the courses I had been taking at the Motherhouse. I went to my old high school where the same nuns were located. I took my finals under their supervision and in this way earned credit for the first semester of my second year of college. I applied at Viterbo College, which was an all girl's college taught by Franciscan nuns of a different Order than the Franciscan nuns in Rochester. All of my college courses were accepted by Viterbo except for the courses in theology. They allowed me to enter at the semester time, which was unusual. I decided to major in art and minor in English. I had a wonderful roommate, named Agatha who was from Hong Kong, China. We became best friends as neither of us drank, smoked or went to bars. I spent a lot of time with all of the other foreign exchange students and a couple of other wonderful girls, Deanne and Ellen.

One day my brother Eddie came to visit me at school. He shared with me all of his problems and when I returned to the dorm, I started crying. I cried so hard that I couldn't stop. My friends took me to see the counselor who arranged for me to see the psychologist in the morning. From that time on I went to see Sister Roderick, the college psychologist, once a week until I graduated. She was very instrumental in helping me through all the difficulties of college life. She brought me to a greater understanding of myself and my problems. It was because of her inspiration and faith in me that I graduated.

Viterbo College was only 25 miles from my hometown, but on weekends when most of the students went home, I stayed in the dorms. Sister Roderick realized that whenever I went home I returned an emotional mess. Since Agatha had to stay in the dorm, it worked out perfectly that we spent the weekends together. Eventually, my art work hit an emotional block. I found it impossible to paint the expressions I wished to paint on my faces. I realized that this was due to my state of inner emotional turmoil. I was advised to switch majors, which I finally did. The second half of my junior year, I switched my major to English and kept art as a minor. It was almost impossible to earn all the necessary credits in such a short amount of time, so I went to summer school. I had always loved reading and writing and did very well with English as my major.

GALLUP, New Mexico

"There is no cliff too awesome nor a stream too swift and deep, nor a haunted hill too eerie, nor a mountain trail too steep for the questing heart to reach or the eager breath to dare." Lorraine Usher Babbitt

The summer following my graduation from college, I signed up as a lay missionary with the Franciscan Missions in St. Michael's, AZ. There I was assigned to work at the Catholic Indian Center in Gallup, N.M. I taught the little Navajo Indian children, aged from about five to eight years. We would go out to the mission buildings in remote areas which were very primitive. The children would slowly filter into the building. We were lucky if we saw the same children week after week. Other missionaries from other religions went to these same places and tried to win the children over to their mission with candy and goodies. The culmination of all of our work was the day on which the children were baptized and received their first communion.

I remember that special day very well. The Bishop came to the Catholic Indian Center. All of the children lined up to be baptized, while I played the organ. When water was poured over the children's heads, streams of mud ran down their cheeks. This was due to the fact that most of the children lived in hogans and did not have access to running water.

While I worked at the Catholic Indian Center, I had the weekends to myself. During this time I had a boyfriend who lived in the city of Gallup. One of the priests, Father Anthony, treated us by taking us to the desert where there was a filming of "The Distant Trumpet" taking place. We had our pictures taken with Troy Donahue, the star of the film.

Father Anthony also took us to visit the jail in Gallup. While waiting in the aisle, I happened to glance back by the prisoners and saw one of the prisoners holding up a piece of mirror by which he was trying to see us. I told the jailer and he immediately went and took this piece of glass away from the prisoner. He later told us that this man was in jail for murder. He was very grateful that I had noticed.

In Gallup, the two priests of the mission talked to me about becoming a counselor at the new Fort Wingate building complex. I had already signed a contract to teach in Franklin, Wis. and didn't want to void that contract, especially since it was my first teaching job.

On some weekends, our mission group would get together for tours. On one such tour, we went by bus to the Grand Canyon. The bus driver warned that unless we were veteran hikers, we should not try to climb to the bottom of the Grand Canyon. That was all I needed to hear. This was a challenge I wasn't about to pass by.

Nothing could match the grandeur of the Grand Canyon. As far as one could see, the immense rocks and hills reflected the most gorgeous and vivid colors, contrasting sharply with the pure blue of the sky. Looking at this panorama of color, only one thought filled my mind—God. God created this vast beauty. The rock formations with their full array of color stretching farther than the eye could see, filled one with the presence of this amazing Creator. The vastness of it was very humbling. It made one feel small and yet, in a sense, it made one feel great—great to be alive and able to experience such a miraculous work of art. It was absolutely breathtaking!

Upon reaching the Grand Canyon, I found two other missionaries as eager as I was to walk to the bottom. We started out about noon, and when we reached the bottom, because the heat was so intense, I started having fainting spells. The two boys who accompanied me cared less and kept right on walking. Left alone, I could have died and they didn't seem to care. Finally, I caught up with them at the Colorado River. All three of us jumped into the river to cool off. Once we got out of the water, our clothes dried in about three minutes.

That night, the two boys wanted to stay at the bottom and sleep, but I objected strongly. I convinced them that we had to climb back up that night. I was worried about my reputation. They agreed to climb back up but only if I carried the water, which I did. Each time we would arrive at a plateau, we would dive head first into the dirt because it cooled us off. By the time we reached the top, which was about 2 a.m., we were totally covered with dirt. When the others heard of our adventure the next day, we became instant heroes. Two of the missionaries told us that they watched us with binoculars and saw a mountain lion following us. If I would have known that, I'm afraid I would not have had the courage to endure.

The three months I stayed in New Mexico, I did a lot of rock climbing. Most likely because of my young age, I was very adventurous and would climb out further on the rocks than anyone else. This was all one great adventure for me. During this time I grew to love the Navajo people. One day, I would be back.

FRANKLIN, Wisconsin

"Keep your faith in all things; In the sun when it is hidden, In the Spring when it is gone." Roy R. Gilson

It was my first year of teaching and I felt I was ready. I had gone through psychotherapy while in college. I had faced the reality that my art talent was not nurtured enough to get me through college and had changed my major from art to English the second half of my junior year. Somehow I had managed to come out with fairly good grades despite the fact that I had pleaded several times with my psychologist to put me in a hospital. She had given me the support necessary to get me through.

I was hired after my first interview and I attributed that to the A+ I had earned in student teaching. My interviewer pointed to a huge pile of applications that he had on his desk, and told me that he was choosing mine.

My new job was to teach art in the morning at the grade school and to drive to the high school for an afternoon of English classes. When I was hired I was told that I would be an assistant in the art department. As it turned out, I was the art department. For English I taught one junior class, high freshmen and low freshmen, which meant three different preparations. In addition to teaching, I was assigned extracurricular activities of GAA and Pep Club.

My enthusiasm paid off that first year. I was told I was doing a super job. Eventually, however, I began to doubt that this was true. I began evaluating my work and felt I could do a whole lot better. So I tried. I spent my entire weekends either at the library or in my bedroom, the room I rented from an older lady in her home. Sometimes I would get caught discussing the lady's many problems, as she was divorced. That was the extent of my socializing.

The teachers were all very friendly and helpful. Some of them thought I should get an apartment where I could share the rent with another and have some companionship. Luckily, there was a teacher who decided to move in with me to an upper flat in the city of Milwaukee.

It was there that my troubles began. The piles of papers were growing steadily. I slept on an army cot at night and had trouble sleeping. I don't know what to blame this on, although my roommate was up half the night with her boyfriend. I didn't realize, until we had moved, that she was a divorced woman. I couldn't understand why we seemed to converse less and less until finally we weren't talking at all. She would take her supper and move to another room to eat. After a while I began to feel insecure about practically everything. Somehow the principal at the high school learned about the fact that I was very insecure. He requested a talk with me and during this conversation stressed the fact that I was doing a very good job and he wanted me back the following year with a substantial raise. I couldn't believe it.

Eventually I talked myself into believing I was doing a terrible job. Yet while in the classroom, everything went smoothly. Once outside the classroom in the halls, the noise of the students passing from room to room became unbearable. Sometimes I would race toward the door, eager to leave the noise behind. On the way back to the apartment I began getting strange thoughts, such as how easy it would be to run my car off the road. This thought grew stronger and stronger, along with the wish to bash my head against the wall, or poke my fist through the window.

I had been going to visit a Capuchin, and when I related my problems to Father Andre, he advised me to see a medical doctor. The doctor advised me to see a psychiatrist, which I did. I can remember very well my thoughts on the way to Dr. Joseph, the psychiatrist. I was strongly tempted to end it by driving my car into a tree.

MILWAUKEE, Wisconsin

"In the depth of winter, I finally learned that within me there lay an invincible summer." Albert Camus

I arrived at the psychiatrist's office very shaky and unsure of myself. This was the last place on earth I wanted to be. He greeted me very formally and asked me what the problem was. I tried to tell him, but I wasn't very open. Evidently he wanted to see just how upset I was because he suggested I take a tranquilizer and asked if I was on anything at that time. When I was unable to tell him what pill I was taking, he began ruffling through his drawer making so much noise I thought my head was going through he ceiling. He kept this up for what seemed like 10 minutes. He then held out his hand and asked if this particular pill was the one. He handed it to me but I was so nervous by then that it flew out of my hand halfway across the room. He continued to place pills in my hand and they continued to fly out. He then gave me a prescription for some medication. Finally he said the interview was over, gave me another appointment and told me that if I had anything too hard to handle during the week I should admit myself to County Superior Hospital Psychiatric Ward.

It happened. The next evening I was alone with my roommate. She hardly said a word. Finally I decided to tell her about my talks with Father Andre' which led to my seeing a psychiatrist. She then realized what I was going through and began telling me she was going through something similar, only her psychiatrist forbade her to say a word about it to anyone. That was why she had been eating her meals in another room. She was very understanding and helpful that night, but it was too late. I couldn't handle the suggestions my imagination was presenting to my mind. I felt I wouldn't be able to control myself much longer. Suddenly I remembered what the doctor had said about admitting myself to County Superior. My roommate helped me get packed to be on my way.

I drove to the hospital alone. Upon arriving, I asked to be admitted to the psychiatric ward but I discovered that it wasn't that simple. I had to wait for an interview with the doctor on duty. Before too long, a fairly young doctor approached me. He looked very pleasant so I knew he was not going to frighten me. The problem was, I looked so well and stated my problems so clearly that he could not believe that I was ill. After talking with me for about an hour, he was even more convinced that he shouldn't admit me. If he would have allowed me to go back home that night, I am afraid of what would have happened. Finally, he asked me if I was taking any medication. I showed him my pills and he made his decision based on the medicine I was taking. He found it hard to understand anyone wanting to get in the hospital as badly as I did.

I expected to be surprised at what a mental hospital was like, but upon hearing the door lock behind us, I wasn't so sure that this was where I wanted to be. I was met by two women aids and taken immediately to the bathroom where they took everything from me, marked it and put it into a locker. They looked me over and exclaimed over the fact that I didn't have any bruises on my body. This remark made me wonder even more why I wanted to be here. After giving me a bath, they looked me up and down trying to figure what clothes they might have that I would possibly fit in because I was very thin at the time. They didn't do a very good job. When I had put the clothes on, I couldn't believe them when they said I looked good.

I was changed into a nightgown and assigned a bed which I warily climbed into. That first night I was in bed without any medication and naturally couldn't sleep all night. I heard screaming coming from another wing with the words "Please help me, help…God help me" over and over again. Just before morning, I must have dozed off because when I wakened I sat up so see where I was. There were three other beds in my room. I said good morning but was completely ignored. An aid came in and told me it was time for medication. My medicine was prescribed by Dr. Jason, the doctor who admitted me. It was liquid Thorazine. When I asked why the medicine was not in pill form, I was told that the liquid has a quicker effect. Soon we were lined up in the hall to weigh ourselves. I didn't see the sense of it but went along with the others to be weighed.

After a silent breakfast, which made me wonder if they also had a golden silence like the convent did, we were left free to wander. Everyone wandered into the recreation room, which was a giant sized room with chairs lining the walls and a few tables in the middle. I noticed briefly that there was a window wall separating us from the doctors and nurses who looked at us like they were visiting a zoo. I tried to avoid the staring faces but there was no spot in the room where one could not be seen.

After a short time of being stared at, the new patients were ordered to line up. We were herded out the locked door and onto an elevator which took us to the X-ray room on the first floor. I was aware of the stares and realized we must have been quite a spectacle, with our baggy clothes and staring faces. I don't know if it was the fright of being in this place or the reaction on the faces of the "normal" people, but when they came to get me for the X-ray, I suddenly felt very sick. Just before she clicked the machine, I vomited over everything. I was rushed out and placed at the back of the line. By the time they had cleaned me up and again came to my turn, I walked in rather sheepishly. They got me ready again and just before they pushed the button, I fainted. This time they placed me in a wheelchair and sent me back upstairs.

Every new patient had to go through staffing before any treatment was prescribed. This consisted of a group of doctors and nurses seated around a table. The patients were brought in one at a time. When it was my turn, I decided I had made a mistake in coming to this mental hospital after all. They asked me why I was there and I told them that I was very inquisitive and wanted to see what a mental hospital was like. They looked at me quizzically and demanded I tell the truth. I repeated over and over that I was here because I was curious as to what a mental hospital would be like. Finally they gave up and sent me back to the floor. As soon as I arrived back on my floor, a doctor following me told me to go into a small room with him. He looked like a kind but serious man. He said the staff realized I was frightened and thought it would be easier if I had only one doctor to face, so I decided to give in and tell him exactly why I had come.

That day the medicine started to work. I joined the rest of the patients in their favorite activity of sitting along the walls and staring into space. For two days I could have been doing nothing but sitting for all I knew. Those two days of my life are completely lost. I didn't even know I was alive. The third day, when I came back to being a knowing, feeling, living human being, I was told I had an appointment with my doctor. I was led into a small room and there I waited.

I was amazed to see the same doctor who admitted me, as he had told me he was the head of third floor, which was the men's ward. Dr. Jason sat down and told me he had chosen me as a patient. He told me he was thankful he had admitted me, as he now realized I was a very sick young woman. We talked for a while and I felt very good that this affable, young man wanted me for his patient. To be chosen like this made me feel as though I were someone special. When I walked back to the recreation room, I noticed my doctor standing with the nurses, all staring out the window. I was sure they were staring at me. I wandered into my room, lie down on the bed and fell soundly asleep. From then on, I fled to my room whenever I couldn't take anymore of what was happening. The other patients informed me that I was breaking their number one rule which was that no one could lie in bed at any time during the day. Yet for some reason, I was allowed to lie on my bed whenever I felt like it. I must have been totally exhausted, as I never slept so much in my entire life.

One morning as I was walking down the hall, one of the patients told me I had received some flowers. I quickly went to the office to see. They were from some of my students. I also received a pair of pajamas from one of the staff secretaries at school. I was told it was very unusual for a mental patient to receive gifts or flowers. I thought that they probably didn't even know I was a mental patient.

One of the first days, I noticed a younger girl, with both arms bandaged to the elbows. I walked over and started up a conversation. It seemed she had just attempted to take her life and that of her baby. I had heard about it on the radio only a few days before. This youngster looked nowhere near the age at which one could have a baby. She had been an orphan and felt that no one loved her. I couldn't imagine anyone feeling so alone in the world, so unloved and so desperate as to want to take her own life.

I dragged out a large puzzle, the largest I could find, and began putting it together on one of the tables in the middle of the floor. I told everyone around me that I planned to be better by the time I finished the puzzle. I was putting together the pieces of my life. Often while I was working on it, student nurses would gather around and eventually I began communicating with them. I looked at my life up to that time. I realized that anything I had ever done was done more for my parents than for myself. I didn't really know myself. In fact, I had never developed the kind of independence needed for one to go into a new world and make a life for herself.

I was so overwhelmed by the stigma of being ill that I wouldn't allow them to notify my parents. I simply would not tell them my parents' names. It was extremely important to me that my parents should never hear about my hospitalization in a mental hospital. My priority has always been to please my parents and make them proud of me. I would never want them to know that I was a failure. They had been so proud of me as their daughter and as a teacher. How would they feel now? They must never know. It didn't bother me that much that anyone else learned of my illness, but if my parents learned of it they would be literally crushed with disappointment and shame.

Dr. Barry, the doctor in charge of second floor, persisted in trying to get information from me. He told me that it was hospital policy to send non-residents (as I was because I had not lived in Wisconsin a year yet) to their own state hospital. I would not give in no matter what they threatened. I felt that it would be the worst that could happen to me, to be sent to my home state where people from home might find out.

I met several interesting personalities in the hospital. There was the woman who had just had a baby. She would walk up and down the hall moaning softly. Sometimes I would walk with her and put my arm around her to assure her there was someone there with her. I myself felt very alone and frightened, but by the time the first week had gone by, I felt like a veteran.

In group therapy, I was introduced to a girl who was a homosexual and had attempted suicide. Dr. Jason told me this later when we were alone. When Dr. Jason had us in group together, he pointed out to her how thin I was, and wouldn't she feel a lot better if she would diet and look more like me? I was sure he was setting me up for an attack of some sort. When I told him how I feared her, that she always seemed to be looking at me, he had her discharged.

There was a woman I could label as my best friend, as she followed me around like a puppy. She seemed very "normal" to me, until I discovered from my doctor that she wanted to get rid of her four children. I would often overhear her discussions with her doctor. Up until then, I had never thought it possible that a mother could not love her own children. This woman wanted to have my clothes when I left, because she felt they gave me better clothes. She, like many others, wanted me to draw her portrait. I had never before been able to draw portraits, but now I walked around with a pad of paper and pencil constantly, seeking out people to sketch. Then I would tear it off and give the sketch to the model. This woman wanted me to draw her, but she was one woman I found impossible to sketch, because her facial expressions changed from a hard, non-caring mother to a nice, companionable friend. I felt unable to capture the real person. I was warned by my doctor not to make any arrangements with her about meeting in the future.

One day I happened to be on the elevator with Dr. Jason when a young girl stepped on. Her arm was bandaged from one end to the other. I asked him what had happened to her and he told me that she crashed her hand through a glass door. I asked him later if he thought she would ever get well, as I had taken a liking to her crazy sense of humor, her odd expressions, and her look of total fear. He told me she probably would never get better. I really felt bad. I realized how lucky I was to be getting better every day.

I knew that I would be in the hospital over Easter vacation. The staff tried to get us into the spirit of Easter by telling us we could decorate the ward. The tables were piled high with art supplies. My friend Karen and I started making paper flowers. When we discovered we were the only ones doing anything, the nurses asked us to try and get some of the older women away from the walls to help. Having taught art, I had a knack for getting people involved. Before long, some of the ladies I had never seen move an eyelash that were now deeply engrossed in creating their own flowers. I even saw a hint of a smile now and then. This was a reward in itself.

It was then that we discovered what a great artist Lily was. After that we wouldn't leave her alone. She sketched me once, in my favorite position, of sitting at the table hiding my head in my arms. We began talking and I discovered that she had many achievements to her credit. She was also a prostitute. I had never met a prostitute before and was very curious. She seemed to be such a sensitive, warm person. I found her on more than one occasion sitting on her bed sobbing with her whole body throbbing to the sounds. I tried my best to comfort her, but the other patients told me to leave her alone as she did this all of the time.

Once, I was sitting on her bed talking with her when she quietly handed me what she called "the story of my life." She said she had written it for her doctor and he'd given it back. I took it to my room where I slowly put myself into another personality and tried to think and feel as she did. I didn't get very far when suddenly Dr. Barry, the head of our floor, came in and asked for it. He said that I shouldn't have been allowed to read anything that she gave me. I had read enough to understand his point.

The second week I was there I was told that I had visitors. Three of the teachers had come after school to visit. While we were sitting there talking, I noticed them eyeing the other patients, many who were far worse than me. I explained that this floor was full of all kinds of problem patients and that all were thrown in together in this diagnostic center. From here people were either discharged or sent to the real "bad" place. As I was talking, one of the patients who was dancing with a broom, wandered over to our group and began talking...I should say, babbling some horrid nonsense. I felt mortified to think my teacher friends saw some of these patients.

One day I noticed a new patient who had her hands all taped up. I asked Dr. Jason about her and he told me she had bitten her hands. I didn't know it then but later, through the help of my doctor, she and I were to be brought together as friends. This was one of the biggest mistakes my psychiatrist made.

Dr. Jason visited with me every day I was in the hospital. He gave me the inside story on many of the other patients. He guided me away from patients who were gay or those who were a bad influence. He knew that I was innocent and naïve, and showered me with care and guidance. Eventually, I grew very fond of him.

Two weeks had gone by and my puzzle was nearly finished. I began asking about my release and was told I was ready. My doctor had noticed how I helped clean the cafeteria after meals, how interested I was in art projects and how cheerful I had been at the mixed dance. However, he had warned me not to have anything to do with the patient who had taken such an interest in me, because he had been involved in incest with his mother. He would not be the type for me, to put it mildly. I agreed heartily. We had gone on a few walks and I entertained the group by throwing snowballs at passing cars. Some of the mischievous real self was coming back.

My doctor released me with the warning that if my car didn't start I would be tempted to run right back. I promised him I was leaving for good. He reminded me to go to Recovery meetings, and told me that if I didn't I'd be in a hospital for the next 15 years. I promised him that I'd go to the meetings at least three nights a week. What I didn't know at the time was that he also attended Recovery meetings. Upon leaving, he told me that I should visit him in his office once a week, which I did faithfully. Unbelievably, he let me see him for free. This should have set off an alarm for me, but it never did. I continued seeing him on a regular basis, and I also saw him at Recovery meetings. After the meetings, he would take walks with me and we held hands. I grew more and more attached to him.

The next Monday I returned to school. I felt as though I were a completely different person. Not only did I feel older but I felt very strange. I didn't have any of the self confidence I once had. I couldn't get my mind and my memory working. My preparations took me about twice as long, and yet, when I'd get in front of the class, my mind would go blank. The noises were still as loud. The students looked as if they were talking about me behind my back.

The days went by slowly. One Friday evening I was asked to chaperone the dance. As I was sitting there, the noises grew louder and louder. I became alarmed and ran to the teacher in charge to tell him I wasn't feeling well and wanted to go home.

The following Monday, I was in the teacher's lounge getting my thoughts together. I went to the door and suddenly, as if there was a huge bag of flour in front of me, I couldn't move. I panicked. I ran to the principal and told him I was quitting. He warned me not to make a hasty decision I might regret for the rest of my life. All I could say was that I insisted on leaving, right then and there. I was sent to the superintendent, where I heard more preaching about how this could ruin my whole life. All I knew was that I couldn't tolerate those horrible feelings anymore. I had to get away from anything that might be the cause. I was more frightened of teaching with all these scary experiences going on, than anything I had ever lived through.

If I would have had some Recovery training behind me, I'm sure

I could have made it. I was soon to discover what nervous symptoms are and how to handle them. Of course, with Recovery three nights a week on top of all the pressures of school, I was doing too much. Once I quit teaching, I devoted all my evenings to Recovery classes and very shortly went to work for Manpower. Here there were no pressures, no tasks which required memory work and no getting up in front of a group and being in the spotlight. I enjoyed doing things like working at typewriters in back rooms, sorting out papers, filing, checking and accounting.

The rest of that school year I worked as a secretary and managed my life well, although I underwent every nervous reaction in the book. I had strong, deep depression, sometimes almost succumbing to the temptations to jump off the bridge which I walked across to get to my Recovery meetings.

One bright spot in my day was running into Dr. Jason, who went to the meetings to help his former patients. I learned later that he also went through the same symptoms of every nervous patient. I looked forward to the comments he made whenever I gave an example, and even more to the gatherings at a nearby bar. Gradually, I began to master my emotions, to direct my thoughts and to regain some of the confidence I had once possessed.

BROOKFIELD, Wisconsin

"In the middle of difficulty lies opportunity." Albert Einstein

By now, I had moved to St. Clare's Home for Working Women. Here I made friends with Mary, among others. Over the summer I looked for a different teaching job. Mary told me about a vacancy at St. Anthony's in Brookfield where she worked as a teacher. I applied for the job of teaching fifth grade and was hired.

Over the summer I tried to prepare myself for this job. I was especially concerned about teaching history, as I had always found history to be difficult. I went by bus to the Marquette University campus to the student union, where I proceeded to make a history outline. I was employed by Manpower over this period of time, but had several days off.

One of the first teacher in-service meetings was held late in the summer. When assignments were made, I learned that they were without a third grade teacher. I quickly considered in my mind the possibility of acquiring that job in place of teaching the fifth grade. It seemed a lot more feasible. I walked up to Father Stewart, the principal, and asked him whether I could change from the fifth to the third grade. He seemed pleased and made the necessary arrangements. Actually, during the summer I had been very frightened about taking on the fifth grade. Now that I would be teaching third grade, I was a lot happier.

49

Throughout most of the year I was quite happy. I had a hard time adjusting to some of Father Stewart's rules, however. One of his rules was to make the children cross their arms whenever they walked down the hall, so that they wouldn't touch the walls. I thought it was ridiculous, but I also felt that it was unreasonable to ask the children to do this unless I did it myself. This was only one example of the strict discipline that was enforced in this school.

As the year progressed, I came to love all my children dearly. There was Gregory, Jeff, Debbie, and little Mark. These children made up for the fact that I had third grade instead of fifth, for they were difficult to handle. But any distress caused by them was offset by some of my other students, like Diane, Alan, Maria, and Timmy. I could go on and on. I was in love with the third grade and the third graders were in love with me. All was going well, or so I thought...

I was still seeing Dr. Jason every Friday night. He never charged me for these visits. One night I felt I needed him. Although it was about 10 p.m., he told me to come over anyway. When I arrived, he asked me to come into his house. I was very frightened and refused but he kept insisting. I kept refusing. Finally, he asked me to come into his car, which I did. We sat there and he held me in his arms for a few hours. I arrived back at St. Clare's about 1:30 a.m. Madelaine, my roommate, was very upset with me. The next morning she told Sister Donna, who was in charge of St. Clare's. She asked to see me and while I was talking with her she made arrangements with Father Don for a counseling session. Father Don was Chaplain of St. Mary's Hill Hospital. He also counseled many of the young women from St. Clare's.

Upon meeting Father Don, I was in for a pleasant surprise. Instead of some stuffy old man who preached morality, I found him to be very personable and completely down to earth. After talking with him for only a short while, he asked me to name the doctor who had so completely overtaken my life. I hesitated, not wanting to defame Dr. Jason in any way. Loyalty was one of my strongest traits. Father Don then promised he would never use my information against Dr. Jason. He begged me to tell his name so that he could save other young women from going to this same doctor.

In the process of talking with Father Don, I began to see the pattern that existed. Dr. Jason had complete control over my life. He dictated what I did with my life in almost every detail. He chose my friends and told me when and where to go with them. He told me to go to Recovery meetings, which he attended, and made contact with me on so many evenings. I went to his office for therapy once or twice a week. In fact, I had quit my teaching job because I couldn't fit everything in.

When I talked with Father Don, he gave me an ultimatum. He told me in strong words that I should choose between him and Dr. Jason. By that time I had come to grips with the fact that Dr. Jason was dominating my life and was detrimental to my mental health. So I stayed with Father Don and stopped seeing Dr. Jason altogether. Father Don said that if I went to see Dr. Jason even once more, he wouldn't deal with me. From what he said, Dr. Jason was harming me greatly by making me completely dependent upon him. It was a difficult decision to make, but I chose to stay with Father Don. I liked his firmness, his clear thinking and above all, the fact that he was a priest. I knew I could trust him.

Ever since I had been ill I was told of the necessity of going to Recovery meetings at least three times a week in order to stay out of the hospital. This requisite carried over the summer and on into the following school year. I cut down my number of Recovery nights, but had increased my dependence upon Dr. Jason. I had been calling him for every little decision. The dependency grew into love. I was really deeply in love with him when my roommate reported me to Sister Donna. That is, until Father Don pointed out to me the terrible danger I had gotten into.

At that time, I was doing a fairly good job of teaching the third graders. Father Stewart, the superintendent, stopped in my classroom often and praised me to the skies. But my third graders were beginning to be quite a challenge. I had five students with quite severe emotional problems. Because I wanted to give the best possible guidance to each child, I went to a series of lectures at the U W-Madison. The type of emotions that were being expressed in my classroom were the very same as were described in the lecture. My biggest problem child was testing me to the nth degree. This was because he needed so desperately to trust in someone and that someone was me.

During this period of time of seeing Father Don, going to UW-Madison and caring for my third grader's emotional problems, I began to feel much too sensitive about everything. It was hard to give up my dependency upon Dr. Jason, hard to handle problems of such great intensity of some of my students, and hard to go to Recovery without making some kind of contact with Dr. Jason who attended most of the meetings. I remember one night I felt especially attracted to him, and wished somehow to let him know how I felt. I was so tempted to poke my fist through the glass window of the door just to let him know how intensely I cared for him.

Before I had ever talked with Father Don, I had called Dr. Jason and talked with him about that evening we spent together. I asked him over the phone if he loved me. He answered, "I love you, but not the love that leads to the altar." Puzzled, I hung up, with his words ringing in my ears. That day I picked up my friend, Christine. As we were on our way to my place, I had an accident. I had been so absorbed in thought, while going over the bridge that I didn't notice in time that the car ahead of me hit ice and slid into the curb. If I had been thinking clearly, I probably would have pulled out to go around the car. Thank God I wasn't alert. In fact, at that very moment I was thinking of my disappointment in Dr. Jason. If I had pulled out, I would have been hit by an oncoming semi. Instead, I piled up on the car in front of me and the car behind me slid into mine. My car was completely totaled.

This one particular day at school, my student, Gregory had been unusually unmanageable. I told him to stay after school so I could have a talk with him. Before I could find a chance to talk with him, he decided to disobey me and ran out of the school so I chased after him. When we reached the front door, Sister Herbert and Father Stewart were standing in the entranceway. Sister asked me what was wrong and when I told her, she lashed out and struck Gregory in the face. I couldn't believe that after all the patience and work with this boy; my work could be ruined by this one cruel act. The last thing in the world this boy needed was to be hit. His problems were too complicated and beyond his control. I couldn't believe that Sister could have been so blind.

That night as I was driving home, I was crying. Suddenly, I came to a stop and the car behind me ran right into my car. The poor man begged me not to report the accident because he couldn't afford to lose a point. Realizing it was actually my fault for stopping without reason, I let the incident pass unreported.

I had talked with Father Don a few times when he told me that I should start going to group therapy with Dr. Arthur. In the meantime, Father Don called Sister Donna, who ran St. Clare's, without my knowledge. He warned her to watch out for me as I might have a bad reaction as a result of having to go to group therapy. I did have a reaction, a very unusual one. That weekend I developed some fierce pains in my lower abdomen. I went to bed and the pain got worse and worse. I asked for a doctor but Sister, acting upon Father's prediction, thought it was merely a matter of my imagination. As I grew worse, I couldn't move out of bed to call a doctor myself and I didn't know why Sister wouldn't call. Finally, the other girls told Sister I was really bad. She came into my room to see for herself. She immediately sent for the doctor. The minute the doctor came and laid a hand on me, I was suddenly all better. The pain was completely gone. I was embarrassed by this incident of a psychosomatic illness.

Eventually I moved out of St. Clare's and into an apartment that I shared with Susan and Madelaine. We had found to our dismay that at St. Clare's our lives were really not our own. Sister seemed to interfere in our lives more than we wished. We were definitely not pleased with the lack of privacy.

So it happened that I went to a movie the Friday evening after the incident at school with Gregory. That night the phone rang for me while I was gone. Dr. Jason called about three times and left a message saying I should call him whenever I returned. I drove to my apartment about 1 a.m., parked the car in the underground locked garage and immediately called Dr. Jason upon reading the message. We had a very strange conversation. He referred to my car several times, asking about how necessary it was, the make and the color. He also mentioned the fact that I wasn't seeing or calling him any more. We talked about the car more than anything else.

The next morning, the second graders were to receive their first Holy Communion. I went down to the underground garage to get my car early. Upon reaching my car, I noticed something very strange. My tires were flat. Part of the engine had been pulled out and pieces were scattered around the garage. It looked as if my car was the only one that had been touched. I could not drive to the first Holy Communion service after all.

I was extremely puzzled. The night before, I had driven my car in and it was in one piece. Now this. I talked to the manager of the apartment building and he confessed that he forgot to lock the garage that night. The big question was who had done this and even more importantly, why? I immediately thought of the strange phone call from Dr. Jason during which time he had asked me so many questions about my car. One question in particular stuck in my mind, "I really needed a car, didn't I?" But why would Dr. Jason do such a thing?

It was true that I had stopped seeing him. Was he upset over this fact that I was now seeing someone else and had dropped him? But why would he be jealous when he told me he didn't love me in the way I wished? How did he love me? He had tried to explain. Maybe I had misunderstood. With all these questions in my mind I decided to call Father Don. When I told him what had happened he gave me instructions to enter the hospital immediately. I knew I wasn't sick so I imagined the reason was that he was frightened and wanted me to be somewhere safe from the man he thought to be quite ill, in other words, safe from Dr. Jason. I was right.

I had talked of Dr. Jason and his relationship with me to quite an extent with Father Don. At one point, I understood that he hurt me greatly by carrying on the dependency relationship to the extent that he did. I placed my trust explicitly in Father Don. I packed my bags and entered St. Herbert's Hospital. I was placed under Dr. Tyler's care. Almost immediately I was assigned to occupational therapy. There I happily started a number of art projects. I was able to attend Mass and I listened very carefully to the sermons by Father Don. He, by no means, forgot that I was there. As the hospital chaplain, he visited me every day. Evidently, he was observing me to see whether or not my tale was a fabrication. He was convinced of the truth of my story and so were the doctors. At the end of the week I received word that I was to be discharged.

I gathered my things together, checked out my toiletries and was walking down the hall to say goodbye to Father Don. I had my clay head in hand to show it to Father. I was very proud of it as it was the first attempt at modeling with clay. I was walking down the hall quite happy and worry free, when I saw Father coming towards me. I took one look at him and discovered a grim expression on his face. He came up to me and told me to put my things away because I would be there a few days longer. I looked at him in amazement. He then told me I had just been fired from my teaching job. He told me that I would have to stay until I could make plans for what to do next.

I couldn't believe my ears. I had been so determined to finish out the year of teaching. Now I had to give up my job unwillingly. Father's expression revealed his understanding and comprehension of my feelings. He insisted upon my having a job before I left St. Herbert's Hospital, or at least a good idea of what I wanted to do. One of the first things I did was to sit down and write a letter to Father Stewart, in which I explained why I didn't get a substitute for that Monday and why I didn't show up for my job. It was upon these grounds that he based his reason for firing me. Both Father Don and Dr. Tyler called him and tried to reason with him. In my letter, I explained that I had had to be sent to the hospital and that I had no chance to call and get a substitute. I tried to give him my idea of a hospital, which was based on my hospitalization at County Superior where we had no opportunity to make any phone calls. I didn't realize that I could have called from St. Herbert's.

Father Don tried to explain to me how a priest could behave like

Father Stewart. He said that it was obvious to him that Father Stewart was jealous because I had taken my problems to him rather than to Father Stewart. Father Don said that he and Father Stewart had been at odds for years. He tried to get me to understand that basically Father Stewart was a good man and most of the time he had a heart of gold, but that there was another side to his personality. He had a serious emotional problem and this was as possible for a priest as for any human being. I accepted his reasons and understood to the best of my ability. I simply had to get another job.

I spent the next two days at St. Herbert's looking at the newspaper ads for jobs. I circled a couple of numbers that I planned to call as soon as I got home. Because of this, I was released from the hospital. I haven't seen Father Stewart since. It was the end of my days in Brookfield. I spent more than one night crying over the loss of my dear third grade students. The irony of the situation was that he had a substitute teacher to take my place and it was because of me. I had brought Becky to St. Anthony's in the first place. She had just left the convent and was looking for a job. Father Steward had her on the staff as an extra. She took over teaching my class.

It didn't take me long to find a job. I applied to be a governess for five children. When I went for the interview the woman, Mrs. Reese, was completely understanding of all that had happened to me and hired me immediately. The family lived in a huge home on Lake Michigan. I stayed at that job for several months. Mrs. Reese encouraged me to go out dancing. At the dance I met Joe, my future husband. We started dating on a regular basis. While working for the Reeses, I applied for a job working as a counselor on the Navajo Indian Reservation. During the summer after graduating from college I had gone out to Colorado and New Mexico as a missionary and had gotten to know the priests very well. It was through their help that I managed to get the job. The government told me that I had sub-eligible qualifications because of the psychology courses that I took in college. I was to work for the Bureau of Indian Affairs for the U.S. Government.

FORT WINGATE, New Mexico

"We are wanderers on this earth. Our hearts are full of wonder, and our souls are deep with dreams." Gypsy Saying

At Fort Wingate, I was a counselor for over 100 Navajo high school freshmen. My office was located in the dormitory, but I chose to live in an apartment separate from the dormitory. I shared this apartment with Lynn, who was the phy-ed teacher. We became great friends.

The Navajo teen-agers were slow about warming up to me. At first they were very distrustful. Eventually they observed that their friends were being helped, and they began to trust in me.

One young girl was afraid to go outside. She broke out with a rash over her entire body, and her friends told her that she was allergic to the sun so she stayed indoors all the time. As I counseled her, I helped her uncover some of the turmoil going on inside of her, and it didn't take long before her rash disappeared. Her friends thought I was a miracle worker.

I also counseled teens that had been raped and abused. Many of the young people were alcoholic. It was my job to take these young alcoholics and talk with them every Thursday night.

When the young people came to Fort Wingate, they were supposed to choose a religion. A few of the teenagers refused to pick a religion. I was put in charge of these youngsters. I discovered that they were very intelligent and were simply following their conscience. Many of these young people felt that they were being unfaithful to their Navajo religion and felt that they would be punished if they chose another religion.

One of my most difficult tasks was when I had to break up a fight between two Indian girls. While they were in the midst of the fight, someone ran to get me. I had to go into the room where they were fighting, all bloody and distraught, and literally tear them apart.

On a Friday night, a dance was held and several of the young boys came to the dance drunk. One of the boys was a freshman from my dormitory. I intervened and asked that the police relinquish him into my hands instead of putting him in jail. They allowed me to take him back to the dormitory. When I walked into his room, I glanced down the hall. Several of the young boys were peering out of their doors to see what I would do to their friend. We talked for a good half-hour, during which time he cried openly. I learned a lot about the many fears of the young Navajo boys.

I worked with some very interesting people. We would get together about once a week to discuss our problems and to share insights. One of these counselors was a woman by the name of Annie. She was an expert in knowing how to handle the many problems we were faced with.

At one time, there was the threat of the black plague. One person had died from it and this was enough to be declared an epidemic. Because the carriers of the black plague were prairie dogs, and there was a prairie dog town directly across the street from us, men came on horses and sprayed poison in all the prairie dog holes. One morning when Lynn and I were walking together, we came across a huge snake that had been poisoned. We decided to play a trick on Annie and carried the snake on a stick and placed it in front of her door. When we knocked, she came out and saw this huge snake. She started screaming. We laughed and laughed, but she didn't think it was so funny.

Another woman, Ruth, had been a counselor with the BIA for

many years. She was a person we could trust to help us with almost any problem. At our weekly gathering, she helped us by telling of stories in her past.

One of my freshman boys constantly ran away from school. He would go to places where the Indians smoked peotie, a harmful drug. It was so dangerous for a young Indian to be walking along the roads at night, that I insisted he tell me the next time he planned to run away and I would take him home in my car. The other counselors agreed that this was a wise thing to do. There were a lot of drunken Indians out on Route 66, where he had to walk.

Eventually, the freshmen Navajos began to trust me and to come to me with their problems. I found that I was becoming very attached to them. It was time for me to make a decision. Would I stay, or would I go back to Wisconsin to get married? I knew that if I stayed any longer, I would never go back to marry Joe.

By the time I was ready to leave for New Mexico, Joe and I had become inseparable. But I was drawn by this great adventure. Also, I wanted to pay my father back for the college loan I owed him before I got married. This was a very good paying job and I felt that I couldn't turn it down. Somewhere in the back of my mind, I thought that perhaps if I were away from Joe I would know for sure if I loved him or not.

During this time, I received love letters from Joe every day. His letters were always the same, "I love you" from beginning to end. After a couple of months, he came to New Mexico to visit me. One of the priests, Father Gerard, owned a trailer and invited Joe to use it while staying in Fort Wingate. He also let us use his car. Because of this, Joe had a wonderful visit. We drove to many interesting sights throughout the countryside. When it was time for him to return, he begged me to return with him. This created a dilemma for me, for I was falling in love with the Navajo people but I was also in love with Joe.

I have to admit that I used my illness to my advantage. I shared with the other counselors my past history of mental illness and expressed my dismay over making the decision. I couldn't just say no to the job. I had to justify it by using the excuse of my returning illness. After five months I returned to Wisconsin and into the arms of my fiancé. I knew that if I stayed any longer, I would never be able to leave, because I was getting very attached to the Navajo children under my care.

MILWAUKEE, Wisconsin

"Seek out that particular mental attribute which makes you feel most deeply and vitally alive, along with which comes the inner voice which says, 'This is the real me,' and when you have found that attitude, follow it." William James

Once back in Wisconsin, I found a job immediately. I worked in medical records at Doctor's Hospital for the next two years. Although I didn't have any special training for the job, I tested out better than the students who had just graduated from medical records.

Joe invited me to live in his home. When I talked with Father Don about this, he discouraged me. He said that even if we didn't share the same room, it didn't look good. So I moved into my own little apartment. We dated for four months before he proposed to me. We were married in May of 1966. At first we lived in Joe's mother's house. This didn't work out well at all. Finally, I invited Father Don over to dinner. I was hoping he would give us his views on what had become a very touchy subject. He told us that we should move out as soon as possible. He said it was hard for any two women living under one roof, but it would be especially hard for me.

We didn't have much money because Joe was in an apprenticeship, and so we searched for a place our budget would allow. We were very fortunate to find a lower flat in a nice area for only $90 a month.

We spent a good deal of time looking for a site on which we could build a home in the future. We found a lot we liked and Joe told me all his dreams. We were able to manage payments on this land, an acre and a half, because of our low rent.

I have to admit I thought Joe's dreams for this home were unrealistic. I really didn't have faith that he'd be able to swing it. He talked of drawing up the plans himself and subcontracting the work. I had visions of him falling off the roof, getting fired, pounding his fingers with a hammer, and on and on. These negative or fearful thoughts completely drowned out any hope I might have had that this would really come true.

But I was extremely happy where we were. Soon I would have to quit my job because by now I was pregnant. I spent all my waking hours dreaming about and preparing for the new baby. It was a challenge to make this house look its' best, but we threw ourselves into the task. Joe painted almost every room. My mother and father gave us drapes for the living room. We bought a used carpet and used couch and chair. We used an old table and chair set for the kitchen. We moved our gigantic bedroom set into the smallest bedroom I have ever seen. We had a wall to wall bed.

Our house was set way back off the sidewalk where garages are usually built. For this reason I never saw the neighbors until spring when I could take walks. I didn't mind the isolation because my baby took up all my spare time. Barbara was born about nine months after our move. She was a gorgeous baby and I didn't have to go far to hear compliments. Everywhere we went, whoever saw her exclaimed over what a beautiful baby she was.

One of my old girlfriends moved into this same area and had a baby the same age as ours. We often visited and took the babies for walks. The people who lived above us were amazed at what a good baby we had, for they said they never heard her crying. She really didn't cry long or loudly. I believe that is because we never let her cry. She could have become very spoiled, considering the way we raised her, but Barbara didn't have it in her to be spoiled.

Life on 49th street was beautiful. We didn't own a TV for about two years. We spent every night enjoying each other's company. We could read, or talk, or just play with the baby. I was constantly finding new little jobs to make the house prettier. I would paint, scrub, or polish and enjoyed my housework. Everything was pleasant and beautiful.

One day I was standing in the kitchen by the sink. We had just come back from Church. The house was a mess because of all the rushing around. I hurried with the dishes so I could plan our meal. As I was standing there, thinking about all the work to be done, it struck me that I didn't have the time, like Joe, to sit down and relax, even though it was Sunday. It hit me that this was to be my whole life, that I was nothing more than a servant to my family. I don't know what brought on this sudden change in mood.

This feeling didn't last long. It's just that it had come once and it would come again. A little of the honeymoon feeling was beginning to fade. Life was becoming a drag. I wanted something new and exciting to happen.

When Barbara was two I decided to continue my education. I signed up for a graduate course in English at Marquette University. This seemed to be the perfect solution. I no longer had time to be bored. I became intensely interested in the books I was studying. My theme papers and term papers absorbed my attention. I began paying a little less attention to Barbara and to Joe.

My teacher was very much taken up with the problems of the Black people. I was very sympathetic with the Black people and their problems. These were the days when rioting broke out and we would hear sirens day and night. Joe became afraid to let me go downtown, while I thought I should be doing a lot more by going to convocations, talks and walks. I grew more and more sympathetic with the problems of the Black people.

One Sunday I was experiencing a real letdown. Joe was not at all sympathetic with the Black people, for he had spent a good part of his life cleaning up after them in his father's apartments, which were rented to Black people and were located in the inner city. I was told often that I didn't know anything about these problems. That Sunday I decided to find out for myself. I was bristling mad at some silly little thing. I simply took off, without telling Joe where I was going. I took the bus and rode it until it let me off in the inner city. I knew Joe would be terribly worried and as I reflected on my actions, I decided it might be wise to call Father Don, just to have someone to talk to. Joe also had decided to contact Father Don to see whether or not I had contacted him. So, when I finally did call Father, he had pretty much the whole picture. He told me I should not run away from my problems. He advised me to return home and discuss them with Joe. He said we should not be afraid to step on each other's toes a little. He was very fond of Joe and most likely sympathetic with him. In fact, when we first became engaged, Father Don had approved of Joe wholeheartedly.

Father Don was like a father to me. I always turned to him in time of trouble. He always gave me good advice. So I heeded his advice this time and started for home. I really didn't learn all that much about the "Black problem". I did, however, see homes and buildings that were in pretty sad shape. I had had no idea as to how bad living conditions were for some of these people.

Before I was finished with the graduate course, I wrote a letter to the head of the English department defending my teacher. It seemed that because of his sympathy for the Black people, he was being let go. I got signatures from all the students in his class and took the letter to the head of the English department. It was my form of protest. The English teacher asked me to see the letter and told me that it made his efforts seem worthwhile just to know what we had done for him.

Joe and I were doing fine in our lower flat until the older couple moved away and a deaf man moved in. He was a young, nice-looking man. He made every effort to be friendly with Al and me. He wrote messages whenever he happened to see us. The problem came when he became a little too friendly. We didn't have the same privacy we once had. It happened that his wife had just died of cancer and he had a 3-year-old son to raise. The son didn't live with him but spent part of each day with his father. Between the two of them, there was so much noise I couldn't stand it. Barbara wasn't getting her sleep. We were waking up every night when he would return from second shift. He was so terribly noisy it started to affect my whole life.

The problem was, how do you tell a deaf man that he's making too much noise? The few times I did dare to make a complaint, he wrote back of all his troubles. This made me feel selfish and guilty. Finally I decided that I couldn't complain any more. So I started to complain to Joe. I tried to tell him how everything was going bad. I'd try a little harder to get used to the noise and invasions of privacy. In other words, I wasn't totally open and honest with Joe about my feelings, which were getting worse all of the time.

At this time I had my second baby, a beautiful little girl whom we named Kari Lynn. Having two babies was quite a challenge at this time in my life. I had always thought Barbara was a perfect child, but when Kari came along, Barbara showed just a little jealousy. Dealing with two babies during this time was almost more than I could bear.

I had the same problem with noise as I had had when I was sick. Noises were magnified horribly. I'm sure that everything sounded twice as loud to me as it did to Joe or even Barbara. Barbara was sick often those first few years. When she was sick and not able to get her sleep because of the noise, I would pick her up and hold her in the window so the deaf man could see what he had done. I'm sure he never got the message. I didn't know of any other way to protest. Anger built up inside me and I didn't know how to release my feelings. Things got worse and worse until finally I decided to talk to my parish priest.

Father Tom was a newly ordained priest, very young and inexperienced. However, he knew how to establish a rapport with people. He was very kind and helpful. It happened that as time went on, I talked to Father Tom more and more and to Joe less and less. For this reason Father Tom asked us to come together a few times. It got to the point where I was accusing Joe of things he didn't even know about. I was imagining many faults that had never been committed. Joe became thoroughly confused as to what I was talking about with Father Tom.

I'm sure that in time Father Tom began to believe Joe and disbelieve me. He must have known something was wrong in my mind but was just too kind to mention it. Finally, things came to a head. I was not trusting Joe at all. One night I walked into the bedroom and told Joe I wanted a divorce. We both wept about it. I went in and slept with Barbara. My problems were much more serious now.

The following night I went to see Father Tom again. As we sat talking I told him I wanted to go into the hospital that very night. I insisted upon this. Father was quite hesitant for it was a Sunday evening and patients were not generally admitted then. But because of my insistence, Father called and arranged for my admittance. Then he called Joe and told him what was happening. I went home, got ready and Joe drove me to the hospital. I really think he was relieved to have me there, for it was an admission on my part that I was not functioning correctly which meant there was hope for our marriage.

WAUWATOSA, Wisconsin

"I will love the light for it shows me the way. Yet I will endure the darkness for it shows me the stars." Og Mandino

This was the beginning of what would be three-fourths of a year in a mental hospital. The doctor who admitted me was Dr. George. The following day he saw me and got all the information. Then a medical physician checked me out physically. The hospital I had chosen was St. Herbert's Hospital because that was where I had gone to see Father Don. Father Don, who had been Chaplain and resident psychologist, was no longer there. In fact, none of the staff I had known were there any longer.

For about a week nothing happened. I spent almost the entire week hooked up to earphones, listening to classical music. In this way I avoided other patients and held on to my sanity with a thin thread. The nurses wouldn't accept this for long. One day the records and earphones were missing. When I complained, I was told to find some other form of recreation.

One day I had just set my hair when Father Tom came in to visit with me. We talked a few minutes when one of the nurses came in and told him I was not to visit with any priests. Until that time nothing really went amiss. I managed to stay pretty composed. But this incident caused me to be very upset.

I was given a psychological test and was told to finish it as soon as possible. I realized what the questions meant but tried to answer everything as honestly as I could. It's a funny thing but until that test everything was pretty much on one level. I was not acting in the least bit mentally ill. Once I completed the test it was a different story. The test seemed to open up to me some means of expressing my illness. Whereas I was not afraid of anything, now I was afraid of everything. Before the test I got along with everyone, after the test I trusted no one. I have an idea that that was the whole reason behind giving me the test. I hadn't found an acceptable vehicle for expressing my illness.

Suddenly, my whole world fell apart. I became mistrustful of everyone. I was extremely afraid of everything and everyone. It was at this point that they decided to send me down to occupational therapy. The moment I entered the room, I began to fall apart. Everywhere I looked there were daisies. There were big daisies and little daisies, daisies spinning around and coming right at me. Then everything went black.

I was taken back to the ward. No one really knew what happened, for I have never told anyone. The first time I've spoken of it is here and now. To me, daisies were more or less a symbol of our marriage. We had daisies as decorations on the wedding gowns and daisies were the main flower in my wedding bouquet. It was a symbol, more or less, of a marriage that had gone so wrong.

The doctor decided I wasn't quite ready for OT. So I was kept on the third floor, where the worst cases were kept. Once a patient starts to recover, he or she is sent to the second floor, which is an open ward. The third floor is a locked ward. There was much greater security for the patient on the third floor, as he or she is seldom left alone. On the second floor, a patient is trusted and can do pretty much what he or she wants to do. Another benefit of third floor is that a nurse is assigned to each patient. It is up to that nurse to provide stimulation for the patient. That is, she will look after the patient, will take the patient to the bathroom for purposes of tidying up, will see that the patient has some project to do, and will be pretty much aware of the patient's doings at all times.

As I was put on medication and relaxed more, I had more nervous symptoms. I cried a lot. I even hallucinated once or twice. But to me the big thing was that I was so very afraid of God. I had to have my crucifix taken down as I was afraid of the power it held over me. In the beginning, I was almost totally unaware of the other patients. Yet as time went on it was easier to talk to and trust another patient than a nurse.

Shortly after I had the crucifix taken down, I was moved to another room. One night I heard a lot of commotion. I noticed that they were taking a patient to my old bedroom. I could tell from the sounds of the nurses and doctors that this particular person had attempted suicide. I thought of the crucifix I had taken down and felt simply terrible that this was the room they had chosen. Half the night I lay awake thinking that if this person died it would be my fault for having taken the crucifix down. He lived, however, and was dismissed for home after about three days.

Overnight, my marriage problems were solved. I realized what had happened, that my illness was the reason for turning against Joe. He also suddenly realized why I had acted so strange. For him this must have been a happy realization, for he loved me too much to believe anything could go wrong with our marriage. I began to count the minutes before visiting time. His visits were like a rescue boat in troubled waters. He was so strong, so vital, and so real. It was I who had been weak and unreal. Things cleared up very quickly as far as our marriage was concerned. Now our only problem was to wait for me to get well.

When I was feeling better I was allowed to go back to occupational therapy. The daisies I had seen were not an hallucination. They were actually there. Many art projects used daisies. I was happy to know they would not bother me again, for Joe and I were once more a real husband and wife. I felt an urge to be totally creative. I wouldn't pick a project that was half done or had a pattern. I wanted to do something I had never done before. My first project was to make a shoe bag. I drew and cut the pattern myself. I spent a lot of time on this article. Time is one thing a mental patient has a hard time dealing with. It seemed that if one could keep busy, the time went much faster.

About this time, I was told I would be there for eight weeks. This crushed me. I resigned myself to it, although I missed Joe, Barbara and Kari so much I often cried. Sometimes I cried for hours on end. I spent my first couple of weeks just crying.

I noticed about this time, that I hadn't had my monthly period since entering the hospital. I told the nurses I thought I was pregnant. They discounted this and told me that it was more likely that my emotional state affected my rhythm. So I put it out of my mind. However, before I forgot about it I wrote a note for my chart. The note said that even if I was pregnant, and taking all kinds of medicine, my fears were that the baby would not be normal. I wanted it known that in no way would I want an abortion.

Shortly after this, one of the new patients came up to me and told me that I was pregnant and that I would have Rosemary's baby. I had not read the book but had been told the story. I knew very well what the woman had in mind, .that I would have a child of the devil. I became extremely upset and reported it at the nurse's station. They assured me that this woman wouldn't bother me again.

Finally I began to notice the patients around me. I began talking to the patients and nurses. This was my first breakthrough on the way to recovery. Once I passed the crying spells, I even began to enjoy certain things.

The hospital offered several means of recreation. One could play cards, make puzzles or work on art projects. There was a piano on third floor and one could play pool if accompanied by a nurse. People could also go outside for volleyball. There was a corn roast and square dancing party one evening. As time went on, we could sign up for outings and go on picnics.

After I began to come out of my shell, I noticed some of the young girls dancing out on the porch. I observed them for a couple of nights and then decided that I would like to express myself by dancing, as they seemed to be doing. When I was young, I tried to do this sort of thing. Then I would pull all the shades down and dance with absolutely no inhibitions. Now I would do the same thing.

I put my whole self into my dancing. I would make sure all the shades were pulled between the recreation room and the porch so that the older patients couldn't see me. The young girls treated me like an intruder at first, but eventually I must have shown them I was only interested in my own self-expression. I moved and breathed the agony I was going through. I became totally absorbed in my dancing. I physically acted out all my mental torture.

One evening, I must have been dancing about a half hour when suddenly I noticed the nurses watching me. It seemed as though they were cheering me on. I began to talk with them in between breaths. The interchange became more and more exciting in my mind. All at once, I saw them coming after me. They each grabbed one arm and began leading me to the bedroom. It seemed as though they didn't understand what I was doing and couldn't accept this physical outburst which I felt was innocent and artful. I fought them all the way into the bedroom. I heard one nurse exclaim that she never thought I had that much fight in me. Then everything was black. They had given me the needle.

One of my friends sent a beautiful plant. When the nurse brought it to me I couldn't believe that anyone thought that much of me. I began to cry, I was so touched. Joe and I were visiting one afternoon shortly after I had received the plant. Our talk was interrupted by a loud crash. The woman who talked to me about Rosemary's baby had picked up one of the plants and thrown it across the room. I remember picking up my plant and taking it to the nurse's room for safety.

While visiting, Joe and I would often listen in to other patients with their visitors. This particular woman who threw plants also poured water or I should say, threw water at other patients. She believed they were wicked and she was driving out the demons by throwing water at them. She was talking very loudly to her husband one day and we overheard her telling her husband that he was wicked and possessed by the devil. We began to understand that as sick as I was, there were others there in worse shape.

Joe would often talk with other husbands on the way in to see me. He told me that one woman had been there about half a year. This

71

woman still had not begun to snap out of her serious illness. She was always moaning about her only daughter who was dead. I always felt sorry for her having lost a daughter, but my husband heard the real story from her husband. Her daughter didn't really die, only in her own mind. She became sick upon having her second baby.

Actually, there were several women in the hospital who had become ill shortly after having their second baby. Another woman, Terry, had just had her second. She was always crying over her behavior, telling us she would be so happy if God would give her just one more child. She was in agony over the fact that she had injured her oldest child. I believe this was true, for she showed me a picture of her daughter, and it did look as though the child was deformed. She spoke of the harm she had done often and with much regret.

There was a great deal of time to just sit around and visit with the other patients. One such morning a new woman was admitted. She was a beautiful young, tiny Filipino woman. She looked as though she was very frightened and uneasy. I was feeling better to the point that I came to care about the others, so I walked up to her and started a conversation. I discovered she was expecting a baby. She had come to this country only recently with her husband who was a doctor. She didn't know anyone and none of her neighbors had called on her. She felt lonely and frightened so I did my best to help her feel at ease. We even had some fun.

Terry had developed a few odd habits, like shrugging her shoulders every once in a while. What was funny was that the new woman followed Terry around and unconsciously did whatever Terry did. I noticed this and told them how funny it all was. After discovering that this is what she had been doing, the Filipino woman laughed at herself. We became good friends in the short time she was there. She didn't stay for long because, according to the nurse, she really wasn't ill but only very lonely and isolated. She was going to go on a trip with her husband and by that time she would be having a baby to keep her company. Before she left, she came up to me and told me I was the kindest person she had ever met.

I wasn't too sick for very long. Eventually, I began to laugh and joke with the nurses and aides. They seemed to enjoy my company more than some of the patients who were always somber and silent. I met a priest patient who seemed to be perfectly sane. I discovered that he was there because he was an Alcoholic, and this hospital also treated that illness. The priest and I became very good friends. He had many stories to tell from his past. He had been a chaplain in the navy. When he returned and was given a parish of his own, people began to invite him for parties, and that was where he started drinking. He knew Father Don when I spoke of him. In fact, Father Don had sent him to the hospital. He was very angry at Father Don for having done this. He always told me to "play it cool" and I'd get out a lot faster. I never knew exactly what he meant.

Every once in a while a patient would go home before getting well. Everyone seemed to know this except the husband. One such experience happened to a woman I had talked with just the night before. We were sitting out on the porch together and one of the teens had put a record on. The song struck us as quite weird and we started to laugh at it. I am not quite sure just why I laughed, but suddenly I could tell the other woman was laughing hysterically and I felt I was the cause. It was obvious to me that this was a sick laugh, not at all normal. That's why I was so surprised to discover that she left for home the following day. I learned that her husband thought she was capable of becoming well at home and thought the whole idea of the hospital was a lot of nonsense. I could imagine what this woman would have to deal with once she was home.

There were many patients whom I haven't talked about simply because they were either too far out or just didn't want to associate with the others. One of these was a woman about my own age who just sat in a chair all day long. She never washed her hair and wore a red wool dress every day despite the stifling hot weather. Her eyes were dark and her face looked ghostly white. Whenever we would go out for a walk on the grounds, the nurses would coax her to go along. She would walk as rigidly as she sat, without looking one way or the other. She ended up going home before I did.

The nurse's aids grew quite fond of me. At meal time, they always sat around and joked and talked with me and a few other patients. There were five young high school girls on third floor. One of the girls was found to be troublesome and her mother sent her to the hospital rather than to a home for delinquent girls. Her mother worked the night shift and therefore, knew what the hospital was like. I couldn't understand why any mother, knowing or unknowing, would send a daughter to a mental hospital.

My roommate was a very young girl, about 16 years old. The day I entered the hospital I was shown to my room. On the other bed lay this girl with beautiful long, blond hair and eyes quite heavily made up. She was wrapped in a wool blanket. This struck me as very odd since it was in the middle of a very hot summer. In fact, I mentioned it to the nurse who told me that despite the weather the girl was always cold.

I never got to know my roommate very well. I only knew that she was sick in a way much different than I. She would often run and laugh for no reason at all. One would see this beautiful figure running as if someone were chasing her, flying through the halls laughing a very shrill, haunting laugh. I spoke to her only a couple of times. I asked her what could have made her sick, seeing how she had such a lovely family. She only said, "These things happen."

One of the young girls was quite studious, very serious and quite distant to any of the other patients. She was always alone. I tried to be friendly with her and she told me that it was my fault that I was sick. When I would mention my daughters, she would say she didn't think I really loved them or I wouldn't be here. I learned that this was really her problem; she felt unloved. Her mother was ravenously beautiful, but the daughter was evidently not impressed. She seemed to be very withdrawn and very full of mistrust.

A couple of the young girls were there simply to keep them off the street. One of these girls was very beautiful and obviously knew it. She was very sexy in her dress, wearing daringly short skirts. I saw her crying a couple of times, but for the most part she looked as though nothing could affect her.

Actually, everyone on third floor was happy when the girls were moved down to second floor. They didn't care who they hurt with their wild behavior. They would run and jump on the couches, switch TV stations, eat in front of the others, scream and yell, and be altogether too noisy and thoughtless. My roommate was not included in this group.

One evening, we were taken to the recreation room for games. I was standing alone, gazing out the window. The room had windows on three sides and one could see all of Milwaukee. Suddenly, I noticed someone standing next to me. She greeted me and as I looked at her, I recognized her as one of my former students. I felt my heart pound as tears welled up in my eyes. She asked me not to feel badly that I was here. She still respected me and realized that anyone could become ill. I still attached a lot of stigma to my being ill. I didn't want anyone to know, especially this young nurse who had once been my student.

We went on a picnic. A bus picked us up and transported us to the picnic grounds. I was in good spirits knowing that very soon I would be going home. I talked with the nursing student who had been my student. I told her I'd pray for her state boards and hoped she'd say a prayer for me.

The picnic was a lot of fun. With the exception of one or two despondent patients, we enjoyed the outdoors, the hike, the lake nearby and the food. After we ate, a couple of women lay down on blankets. I didn't have a blanket but even lying on the ground I fell fast asleep. I couldn't imagine how I had gotten so tired. I began to wonder if I was pregnant.

I was in the hospital about four weeks before I was permitted to see my children. It was really the first time I had ever been separated from them. One day, the nurse on the ward told me the doctor had written on my chart that I could visit with Barbara and Kari. As the day wore on, I was anticipating this reunion with much joy.. Finally visiting hours came. I was waiting with much anxiety and mentioned this to one of the nurses. She went to check my chart and reported to me that yes, the doctor was allowing the visit but that no one had called to tell Joe. I couldn't believe that something so important to me could have been overseen by a nurse's carelessness. I ran out to the nurse's station and started pounding on the window, screaming at them to get my babies. The nurses were astounded at this outburst from someone as quiet and orderly as me. As soon as they discovered this oversight, they called Joe and told him he could bring the babies along. I waited with such anxiety and fright that it seemed harder to wait for them than when they were born. Finally Joe came and brought Barbara and Kari with him. From then on Joe was allowed to bring the girls into the hospital.

There was one lady on third floor who remained somewhat a mystery to me. She seldom had any visitors. She was in a wheelchair and had never been out. In fact, whenever she wanted to go somewhere she would mutter a few sounds because she couldn't move herself, being that her arm was bandaged and in a sling. I usually noticed her sputtering a few sounds and would do what I could for her. She began to count on me, and I became her helper. Whatever her tragedy, she had done something to herself which had completely immobilized her and struck her dumb. She actually looked like a very fine lady, the type of woman one associated with a big horse ranch, dressed in the finest clothes, married to a very successful man and having a couple of dutiful children. This was only true in my imagination. Actually, I saw her with a visitor only once, and this was her son. I never did hear her story.

I grew to know most of the patients and their individual stories. We would have group therapy during which time a few patients would reveal their story. It seemed just at the time I grew more secure, more at ease with the third floor people and nurses, I was transferred to the second floor. It was as though the staff didn't want a patient to feel too secure. This was a signal that the patient was not really gaining anything and had arrived at a certain plateau on the way to mental health.

I'll never forget the day I was transferred to second floor. Terry, the woman who had "harmed" her baby, had grown quite attached to me and quite secure in the fact that we were always together. When I was transferred she was moved down to second floor shortly after.

Evidently, she was not yet ready for this floor, where one had much more freedom. I saw her being carried back up to third floor screaming, kicking and fighting as a result of having had a terrible time adjusting. I was told she would be much happier back on third floor. This made me realize that I evidently had progressed quite far to be able to make this big step with so much ease. I knew that it wouldn't be long before I would be released.

By now I had almost completely forgotten my fears of being pregnant. At mealtime I was eating much better, in fact, the men were complaining that I put down more food than even they ate. Evidently the nurses also began to wonder and finally ordered a pregnancy test for me. By this time I was doing so well that I was being prepared to return home. The nurses told me that my eyes were much brighter and I was much better. Finally the day came when I would be released. I was in my room packing my things when one of the aides came into my room. He was one of my favorite aides, very sincere and kind. He told me to sit down as he had some special news for me. I was pregnant. I would be taken off of all my medicine. I could go home, as planned, or if this were too much of a shock for me, I could stay a couple of more days.

I reacted with much enthusiasm and assured him I would be okay, that I wanted to go home. I was shocked but nothing would keep me from going home to Joe, Barbara and Kari. So I bravely departed.

WAUWATOSA, Wisconsin II

"For three things I thank God every day of my life: thanks that He has vouchsafed me knowledge of His works; deep thanks that He has set in my darkness the lamp of faith; deep, deepest thanks that I have another life to look forward to—a life joyous with light and flowers and heavenly song." Helen Keller

I left on a quiet Sunday afternoon. I said goodbye to everyone I knew and couldn't have been more cheerful and happy. When we arrived home, I could see the neighbors looking out their back porches. I casually said hello as if nothing had ever happened. I'm sure they expected to see something quite different.

Joe dropped me off at home and went to pick up the girls. What a meeting that was! I had my family back again, to love and care for. I tried to do everything at once: wash clothes, clean the dust off and make a meal.

The girls were fussing and crying and I almost turned around and walked back into the car. Joe was very helpful in quieting the children, and I began to feel more comfortable.

After being home a few days I noticed nothing had changed concerning the noises from above. Here I was back in the same situation that sent me to the hospital. On top of everything else, I was pregnant. It was obvious that I needed some kind of help if I was to

78

maintain a state of good health. Father Tom suggested going to a man whom he had observed during his training in psychology. He recommended him highly, saying if I could only get in I would be greatly helped. Joe called and made an appointment. He was Chaplain of Queen's Hospital along with being a psychologist. His name was Dr. Gregory.

I began to feel quite uneasy about being home alone with the children. The time went slowly and I began to wonder what to do to make time go more quickly. I couldn't get myself motivated. I grew very careless about keeping the children clean, much less myself. I lost all interest in housekeeping. It was extremely hot outside and we were forced to buy an air conditioner. I stayed locked up in the house because of the heat outside.

I turned to my sister-in-law for help. I would call her and tell her about my suicidal thoughts. She would immediately invite me to her house, feeling that if I had company I would be all right. I would be fine while visiting, although even there I would go and lie down on the couch. When I returned home, however, I would start getting so depressed I hated to walk through the front door. I couldn't understand why the doctors had never discovered my reason for getting sick. Here I was, back in exactly the same situation. Again I tried to convince Joe to move, and again I failed. I wasn't being truly honest with Joe. I knew we had to move if I was going to get well, but I didn't have the courage to ask this of Joe knowing he didn't have enough money.

It wasn't long before I was unable to stay home alone. Without any medicine, my nervous symptoms were becoming unbearable. I had suicide on my mind from morning to evening. Joe stayed home with me for a few days, but eventually had to go back to work. I became more and more depressed. Joe contacted Dr. Gregory to see what he thought of the situation. He suggested that I return to the hospital because I was very depressed. He thought that they had let me out too early.

What he didn't realize was that I had been cut off of all my drugs immediately after they discovered I was pregnant. After having been on medication for eight weeks, this was a rather sudden withdrawal. Now I was not only mentally ill, but I was pregnant on top of it.

I could not lift my black mood, nor could anyone else. Joe finally called the hospital and made arrangements for my return.. He admitted me under the same doctor, Dr. George. Once again I was on third floor. I was put in the dormitory that was completely empty. This is where they put all new third floor patients until they decided which room would be most suitable.

Upon awakening early the next morning, I was sickened at the thought that here I was back in the hospital. Everything looked black. I had gone home and had not been happy. I was back in the hospital, which I hated. The doctor told Joe I would be here for at least another eight weeks. I couldn't bear the thought. The hardest part of being depressed is that it seems as though it will be forever. There is no hope that one day it will be all over. There is no hope for the present and even less hope for the future. I could see our family getting further and further into debt. My dreams of eventually moving out of our flat seemed farther away than ever. I imagined God had made a big mistake in creating a world that seemed so impossible. The more I thought about it, the blacker things looked. I had only one thought—to escape from my fate by committing suicide.

I pushed a chair under the doorknob and picked up another chair. I started knocking this chair against the mirror hoping to get a sharp piece of glass. The mirror wouldn't break no matter how hard I pounded. Soon I heard the aides at the door trying to get in. They managed to get the door open quickly and saw what I was doing. They didn't guess at what I was trying to do. They thought I had grown to be violent. They put me in a bed across from the nurse's station, tied me down with straps and gave me a shot. The next moment I was fast asleep.

My mood had become so much worse than the first time I was hospitalized. This time it was deep depression that brought me in. I cried day and night. I wanted to be left alone. I walked the halls, looking for a way to get out. As badly as I had wanted to return, I now knew my mistake. I wasn't happy here either. I blamed God for creating me. I wished with all my heart that I hadn't been created for the world was too hard a place to live in. It wasn't long before all my thoughts were directed toward one purpose—to commit suicide. I lived in the hope that I could escape both this world and the next. I simply didn't want to exist.

I'm sure that no one suspected my thoughts of suicide. The aides remembered me as a cheerful, loving person. They trusted me more than they should have. I often walked back to my room to cry alone. They would leave me alone for periods of time. They tried to get me to do something rather than to just mope around all day. They encouraged me to go to the art room to start a project. As much as I had once loved working in the art room, now I wanted no part of it. I would look from one to another project and would find an excuse for not trying it. I just wasn't interested. I looked upon this as one more failure to fit into God's world. In God's world you were supposed to love art. I didn't.

This time I didn't have the benefit of being on medication. I was pregnant. It's funny that with thoughts of harming myself I never considered the possibility that I would be killing my baby as well.

One morning the nurse's aide took me to the bathroom to wash up. Each day my toiletries had to be checked out and checked again upon my return. The aide who came along with me was a very cheerful person. She had taken a liking to me before, and treated me as though I were the same person. What she didn't realize was that I was different. My thoughts were all dark and hateful and I cared for no one. Upon returning to my room I discovered that I still had my deodorant bottle. Without a second thought, I crashed the bottle against the radiator and used the edge to cut both of my wrists. There was no hesitation whatever. My only wish was to die. Later I was told that from the looks of my scars, I had meant business. I looked down at my wrists and saw they were all bloody. I held them in front of me and walked into the hall. Upon seeing me, the nurses were astonished. They acted very quickly. One nurse came to me, one nurse rushed all the other patients into the day room and one nurse called the doctor. They put me in a wheelchair and I was rushed to surgery. The doctor, Dr. George, made only one comment: "You'll never succeed this way." From that time on I was determined to succeed.

My husband was called while I was in surgery. When I returned to third floor I was surprised to see him waiting for me. His face was pale, his eyes uncomprehending. He walked to my bedside and talked quietly, asking me if I didn't love him. I didn't know how to answer, because I realized I was hurting him as much as I was hurting myself. He tried to reason with me, but I could see a look of resignation as though he finally realized just how sick I actually was. He and the doctor chatted in the hall before he came to say goodbye. He promised me he would be in to see me at the next visiting hour. I knew he would come because he hadn't missed one visiting hour yet.

Of course I was given a shot and fell asleep. Upon waking, I was surprised to see someone sitting next to my bed. I was told that a nurse would accompany me at all times. They weren't about to trust me again.

Naturally every patient wondered what happened when they saw me. Someone was always asking me if my wrists hurt. The strange thing was they hardly hurt at all. Even while I was actually cutting myself my feelings were completely nil.

That night, an hour of recreation was planned to take place. Second floor patients were invited along with the third floor patients. I felt uneasy about meeting these patients who were well on their way to recovery. I tried to remain in the background but noticed the looks of the patients I had known from before. The priest I had met came up to me. He looked at my bandaged hands and then at me. "I thought I told you to play it cool," he said. I wanted some sign of forgiveness by God. I asked him if I could go to confession and he willingly obliged. He was just giving me absolution when a nurse came up and grabbed him by the arm. I heard her harsh words telling him he knew he wasn't supposed to do what he had just done. I felt much better, however, for I knew a priest is a priest no matter where he is. My conscience was at peace.

It wasn't long before I got back in the routine of things. There were activities provided for us almost continuously. Right after dinner, there was a rest period, during which time we could go to our rooms and lie down. Every day I waited for this time, as I could shut out of my mind my dark thoughts by lying on my bed and shutting my eyes. At night I was the first one ready for bed. I always wanted to sleep for then I wasn't thinking. I still had only one thing on my mind - suicide.

Eventually I was left alone, as there just weren't enough nurses to be able to spare one for me alone. I seemed pretty much back to my old self, at least I tried to make them think so. I even went out to recreation for walks, croquet, and volleyball. Everything I did was with great effort, for I wanted to be non-existent. Time hung over my head like a deep, dark cloud, and I lived under its' shadow.

As soon as my arms were healed, I was able to play volleyball. However, if I would catch the ball it was very painful. I'm sure this effort impressed the nurse's aides. Usually there were three or four aides with us. One day all the aides were taking part in the game. They played with great intensity. I saw my chance and ran off alone. No one had seen me. Once I was down the hill and out of sight, I broke into a frenzied run. I ran as though my life depended on it. Suddenly I heard voices behind me. I stumbled and fell, hitting my knees on the pavement with great force. My knees hurt to this day from that fall. I hardly realized I was pregnant. The first issue the aides discussed with me was to be careful for my baby. The aides each grabbed an arm and forced me to walk back. I was taken to my room and once again they gave me the shot so I could sleep.

No one realized to what extent I wanted to leave the hospital. I felt that I had made a big mistake by coming back. I knew I wasn't happy at home and I didn't know where I would rather be. Actually there was no place on earth I would rather be. I wanted to leave so I could end it all. I was living in a deep chasm, where no light showed, and no person was near. There were people all around me, but this time I didn't care. I avoided people. I did nothing to occupy my time. I counted the very seconds until visiting time. I would give Joe no rest trying to convince him that I should leave. He talked to Dr. George about my wish to leave and was told it was out of the question. He didn't want me to speak of it to Joe anymore, and if I did, he would cut off Joe's visiting altogether. I didn't stop talking about it but made Joe promise not to tell. If I didn't have him for that small amount of time each visiting day, I would have absolutely nothing to live for.

I was still having my sessions with Dr. George. I knew he felt it was useless to have these sessions. He acted like he was bored to death. In fact, he wouldn't even turn off his noisy air conditioner because it was impossible for him to hear anything I had to say. I begged him to let me go home, but he consistently told me no. He said that if I left St. Herbert's it would be a matter of hours before I would end up at County Superior Hospital and that it was a snake pit compared to where I was now. In fact, he said that if I wouldn't stop begging, he would take me to court and have a judge commit me. I left his office with shattered hopes and feeling completely abandoned.

I went to my room, shut the door and picked up a chair. This time I tried to break the window by reaching the chair legs through the bars. The nurse's aids came in shortly and of course the doctor was notified of this action. I learned later that he thought this was done out of anger. I let him continue to believe this. I was told I had a visitor but under the circumstances, she was advised to come at a different time when I didn't feel so hostile.

I was able to go along to the group therapy sessions. I didn't feel like taking part but listened intensely as the other patients talked, trying to discover if anyone else had ever felt as I did. I felt uneasy, because I was, getting very fat from my pregnancy and still had bandages around both wrists. There seemed to be a hostile attitude towards the group therapy. The only ones who spoke were June, who had a deep crush on Dr. George, and one new patient who informed us that since she was a journalist, she was going to take notes on different patients during the session.

I was the only one who spoke up against such a thing, but I felt as though I were expressing the feelings of the group. I said I certainly didn't want anyone taking notes, since I would be easy to identify as I was the only pregnant patient. The rest of the patients nodded and grunted in sympathy with me.

As the session went on, one of the ladies spoke of being afraid of God. Dr. George looked at me and said that was a problem for me too, and asked if I would have anything to add. I felt a surge of anger to think he would reveal my illness to the others. Actually this is how patients benefit from group therapy, by sharing inner fears and hidden angers with others and realizing that others have experienced similar feelings. Out of anger, I stood up and walked out. No one followed me.

I walked down the long, dark corridor. Instead of turning left to go up the stairs, I decided to go through the doors leading to the front entry. I couldn't believe it—the front door was open and there was no one in sight. I simply walked through the front door and down the steps as if I were any visitor just happening to pass through. As soon as I was outside I started to run. I ran about a block before I looked back to see if anyone was following. A group of about three were coming after me. I could slowly feel them gain and tried to find a place to hide. In my shape they easily caught up with me, and , as before, grabbed me by the arms, and then started walking me back. I had failed again. From that time on I would never see a door unlocked. I could no longer hope to escape.

Instead of getting better I continually went into a deeper depression. I cried all day and all through visiting hours. I wanted nothing more than to die, and my mind was continually trying to think of a way to end everything. I would watch the nurse's station hoping to get the medicine out while they were passing it to the patients. I don't think anyone was aware of my black mood. It was probably hard for the aides to comprehend simply because I had been such a good patient the first time. I had always been able to wear a mask and hide my true feelings. In a hospital, however, this was a little harder to do, because they were constantly doing things like taking your blood pressure, and filling tubes with your blood. I probably didn't fool them as much as I thought I did.

One morning at breakfast, I suddenly got an inspiration. I very quietly left the breakfast table and headed toward my room. I picked up the mop and made it look as if I wanted to clean my room. No one followed me. No one seemed to take exception to my actions. If anything, they thought I was feeling better and doing something positive. Before long they heard a loud crash. I had taken the mop and knocked down the light fixture. I reached for a piece of glass and found a circle shaped piece with razor sharp edges. I inserted the glass into the pit of my arm and dug as deeply as I could to get the artery, remembering my failure the last time. The blood immediately gushed out in a stream. It shot up and over my clothes and over the bed. There was blood everywhere. Just then a nun happened to be passing by and heard the crash. She came into the room, took one look at my arm and quickly made a tourniquet with the pillow-slip. She talked to me quietly and lovingly. I could see that she felt the deepest sympathy, knowing that this wound told of the deeper wound in my heart.

Once again I was wheeled in a chair to the surgery room, and once again Dr. George was called in to stitch the laceration. I judged from his expression that he felt that this was a menial task, something he should not have to waste his time on. He was very curt and quiet. He made no effort to speak to me, as though he felt I was not a real human being only a mental patient.

No one called Joe and told him about it until later that afternoon. Joe came immediately to meet with the doctor about my situation. I could hear them talking in the hall. Dr. George was telling Joe that something had to be done before I ended up killing myself and my baby. They decided to contact Dr. William, my obstetrician, to check and see what medication would be safe. Joe told me all of this later. When he came in to visit me I took one look at his pale, frightened face, and I could tell he was crying inside. I think I improved in that short moment, enough to feel what Joe was feeling, and enough to know that it was entirely my fault.

Time heals. I spent a great deal of time doing nothing but healing. I couldn't get enthused about anything long enough to get my mind off myself. But eventually I started taking walks again. I started working on a rug. I forced myself to do my personal laundry for which each of us was responsible. I got to the point where I couldn't motivate myself enough to take a bath. It seems I had some sense of self-pride, however, because the first time a nurse came up to me and said she was going to bathe me, I realized just how bad off I had become. I decided that from now on I would be more conscious of my daily needs.

Actually, I should have been on medication all the while. Dr. William told Dr. George that the medication I should be taking would not be harmful to the baby. I knew I couldn't live without it. At this time I had attendants with me day and night watching my every move. They never left me alone.

When the time came for me to deliver my baby, I was determined that I would deliver her in a normal hospital and not in a mental hospital. I had to convince Joe to get me out. Time and time again I would beg him to get me out, but he was afraid. Finally I convinced him. We decided to trick Dr. George and scheduled a meeting with another psychiatrist for a second opinion. Dr. George gave me permission to see Dr. James but little did he know that we didn't intend to return.

The following weekend we planned that I would leave. Joe told me not to tell anyone but to simply to sign out at the door. I acted as though everything was OK, but slyly readied my clothes and things for the quick exit. When the nurses discovered I was leaving against medical advice, they tried to talk me out of it but I was finished with this hospital. I didn't feel that it had done me any good; I felt terribly oppressed here. I believed that just having my freedom back would be enough to help me and eventually cure me. I was right.

GERMANTOWN, Wisconsin

"Compassion for yourself translates into compassion for others."
Suki Jay Munsell

Dr. James gave me the OK for staying home. It was very dangerous, but I wanted so badly to be out of the mental hospital so I cooperated fully. Before long, I delivered Anne Marie at St. Joseph's Hospital. The delivery went well and soon I was back home with my baby. Although still very depressed, I made slight improvements daily. In the beginning I didn't move off the couch. Joe had to change and feed the baby. But before long I became interested in caring for Anne Marie. She was such a happy baby smiling all the time. Her happiness gradually brought me out of my depression. I don't know how I did it, but before long everything was back to normal.

I don't remember this time in my life very well. I know that I went back to Dr. Gregory and also went to see Dr. James. Somehow between the two of them, I walked the thin tight rope to mental health. We moved, and this new start gave me the tools and opportunity to live again. I had my third baby. The first few weeks with a new baby weren't too ideal I'm ashamed to say. I could have been just as happy not to even look at her, much less feed, change and bathe her. I'm afraid she got shortchanged when it came to baby care.

In about three weeks, however, I began to change. I began to acknowledge the fact that there was a baby and she was mine to care for. I grew to love her very quickly. I'm sure that this is what helped me to eventually snap out of my depression. The children needed me and the baby couldn't live without me.

Spring came. I met my neighbors, and the children went outside to play. I still spent a good part of my day on the couch, but I had won the first battle. As much as I was tempted to commit suicide, I kept meditating on hell, which was the key to my staying alive. Finally I decided to do little things around the house. Upon looking back, I don't know how Joe ever tolerated me for I was a sloppy housekeeper and a poor cook, but evidently he appreciated having me back so he didn't notice many of these things. I remember finally cleaning the faucets in the bathrooms and kitchen. Once I started cleaning I looked around and found more things which needed doing. I achieved a certain amount of satisfaction in doing work. I slowly started getting up off the couch each day and doing maybe just one more little task.

I complained of being bored often, but gradually realized that my boredom came from being lazy. I knew that if I were to keep the house as clean as it should be, I wouldn't have enough time to be bored. So little by little, I talked myself into mental health. I stopped seeing Dr. James simply because I couldn't stand to wait the three or four hours that was necessary to finally get in and see him. He was certainly a popular doctor.

Little things stand out in my mind like going shopping one day for a birthday present. I realized that it was actually fun to drive into town. And then in church, I would look around and wonder if anyone else had as much trouble washing their hair as I had. I started eliminating my negative thoughts and began to go once more to Recovery meetings. I wasn't too happy with the particular group and so I didn't benefit as much as I could have, so I stopped going. I was seeing Dr. Gregory and this began to take shape as a very important part of my life.

Once the warm weather came and I could get outside to meet my neighbors, I began to achieve more and lie around less. Of course having a new baby to take care of kept me from being too lazy. Gradually I began to take her for walks, visit the neighbors and become increasingly attached to my little Anne Marie. Before long I took an interest in little things such as shopping, visiting the zoo, and going to the Mitchell Park Conservatory, attending Tupperware parties and even joining a knitting club where I learned to knit my first poncho.

I got along for quite some time without any doctor at all. I was notified that Dr. James was no longer in practice, and so I would have no one to prescribe medicine. That didn't even bother me. Eventually I felt a need to be getting some sort of counseling and began to see Dr. Gregory once again. He was just as charitable and attentive as ever.

I can picture myself driving off to see him, speaking to my neighbor of his appointments and taking great pleasure in having someone to talk with. Eventually, however, I found myself being dragged into a little too much counseling. I talked to Father Don asking if I could again see him. It was impossible as he was no longer in that position but a pastor of his own parish. He suggested I go and see Father Earl as he felt Father Earl was one of the best counselors and men in that field. Father Earl happened to be the pastor of our parish. I started making regular visits to him, as well as to Dr. Gregory. They learned of each other through me, and even got in touch with each other. I had a great spiritual need which was fulfilled by both. Father Earl often prayed over me when I would make a telephone call to him. Dr. Gregory gave me a book that explained just how he hoped to heal me, through both a spiritual means and a psychological approach.

As I look back on it now, I can see myself getting more and more involved in self-examination. Perhaps if I had just gone about acting normal and acting completely on my own, I could have avoided what was about to happen.

I took great pleasure in talking with both Father Earl and Dr. Gregory. No way did I need all of this attention. I started writing out my feelings of fears, joys and thoughts. Almost daily I sent a letter to

Dr. Gregory or talked to him on the phone. No matter where he was or what he was doing, he always answered my calls. Father Earl always did the same. I was weaving a web of friendship that soon became my own trap. They say that once a woman loses the joy of her household tasks or of raising her children and begins to spend more time on the phone or writing letters, that this is a sign something is wrong. I started to want to escape from my role as mother and homemaker. My three children were so much work and responsibility I felt that I had to get away from them now and then. I decided it would help a great deal if I could get Barbara into school and have only two at home. Father Earl was more than happy to oblige me saying Barbara could go to St. Mary's school for free if she would only submit to some testing. One of the nuns came out to our house and gave Barbara some tests. She discovered Barbara's age and decided it would be far from the right thing to start her in the first grade. Barbara was only four.

To this day I can't understand what was in my mind that I would have wanted her to start school at an early age. I can't imagine how Barbara could have been any problem, rather than the bundle of joy she really was. I guess the responsibility of three children proved to be a little too much for me at this time because of their young ages. I hadn't reached that maturity that is necessary for a woman to be a good mother and wife.

Father Earl thought a lot of me and at this time asked if I would be CCD (Catholic Christian Doctrine) Coordinator. He said he realized that at this time I had a few problems, but that he was sure by the new school year I would be OK. He wouldn't take no for an answer. I couldn't understand how he could have judged me so wrong. I knew I could never take on this task. He felt it would do me good to have a job and earn some money. I never realized how demanding of a job that would have been. At least I was smart enough not to take it. It was actually a full time job, and paid very well. But at this time I was already over-burdened with my own house and family.

I tried very hard to make friends in the neighborhood. The children played with all the other little ones in the area, and I got to know the women in my block, although there was not one single woman to whom I could talk with confidentially. Everyone seemed rather distant as far as sharing problems. I guess I began to feel a greater need for conversation. My phone calls to both Father Earl and Dr. Gregory increased. Every day started out with a long letter to Dr. Gregory. I was seeing him once a week and he charged absolutely nothing for his services. I began to get so engrossed in my talks with him that I hated to leave.

About this time, Joe decided it would be good for me if we could get away from the children for a little second honeymoon. His mother took the girls and we checked into a big motel in the city. We really lived it up for those three days. I certainly did benefit from that time away. Joe and I seemed to gain back some of the intrigue of our marriage and renew ourselves in our loving relationship. I believe that this came a little late though, for it wasn't too long afterward that I began to slip back.

My neighbor was going to school to become a lawyer. He had one of his first term paper assignments to hand in and was looking for someone to type it up for him. His wife asked if I would do it for $10. I agreed but didn't realize that it was due the next day. I typed morning and night and the effort and worry it caused me must have been that little something that proves to be too much for a nervous patient. The following day I was so out of sorts that I needed some help. I was at the breakfast table, trying to break myself in for the day and felt completely lost and depressed. I don't know whatever possessed me, but I felt such a need to talk I decided to call to have a policeman sent over to talk with me.

To someone else this may seem highly irregular, but to me, who counted on conversation to save me from the dread depression, it was the most normal thing in the world. Two policemen came over and sat at the breakfast table with me trying to figure out just why I had sent for them.

They were very friendly, gentle and kind to just the right degree. I talked easily and trustingly. They asked me what church I went to. I told them, not realizing that they planned to get my pastor to talk with me. I imagined they had better things to do than sit and talk with a mildly depressed young lady. I had to leave to go to the bathroom and didn't realize then that they took this opportunity to call my pastor, Father Earl.

I hadn't realized just how afraid I had become of the strong relationship between Father Earl and myself. He felt he was really doing me good by his kindness and interest, not realizing that he was frightening me terribly. I was always drawn to priests, probably because they were always so charitable and helpful. I was beginning to fear that our relationship had gotten a little too friendly. When I heard a knock, I opened the door, and there stood Father Earl. I was thrown completely into a fearful and dreadful mood. I had been calm and quiet with the friendly policemen because they were strangers. Now I couldn't hide my fear and dread because here was a man who knew me in a much deeper way. I backed away from Father's warm and friendly urging and actually shriveled up in fear. Father was certain I would be able to relate to him, so he sat on the couch and told me he wouldn't leave until I opened up to him.

I ran upstairs and heard his voice follow me, "Don't do anything, Dianne." The fact was, I didn't plan to do anything. I was just a little overwhelmed at seeing all of this attention. Suddenly there was another man at the door. It was Joe. Our neighbor had told Joe at work that there were two policemen at my door, and Joe had come rushing home wondering what had happened. When he entered and saw two surprised policemen and Father Earl sitting in the living room, I'm sure he must have been very frightened. There was no need, however, for I was really OK. I had just needed someone to talk with.

Finally Joe took over and sent both the policemen and Father Earl on their way. Eventually he went back to work, probably very disturbed and upset. That night when he came for supper, I was still having problems. I felt the urgent need just to get away. I grabbed Joe's keys and was going to jump in the car and drive away when he caught me. I told him I wanted to drive where no one would ever find me. This worried him, so he finally turned to our good friend, Dr.

Gregory. He told Joe that my actions prompted some kind of immediate attention and recommended that Joe take me to the hospital again. Joe had just about arrived at the same conclusion.

We both decided against St. Herbert's and Dr. George, and since Dr. James had quit, we had no one to turn to. Joe decided to give Dr. William, my OB, a call and see whom he would recommend. Dr. William told us to go to St. Michael's and try to get Dr. Jeffrey. Joe called and somehow was lucky enough to get Dr. Jeffrey to take me on as a patient. This was always so hard to do because the good psychiatrists had more than enough patients and hated to take on anyone new. So here I was, packing my bags once more, knowing that this was the right thing to do.

I would like to explain my behavior a bit further during this time in my life. As I went to visit Dr. Gregory, I had gradually become more and more drawn to him as a person. He is a small, middle aged man with gray hair down to his neck and in no way handsome or attractive. But to me he was the kindest person I had ever known. He couldn't say no, and he was doing his utmost to help in any way he could. At one of the latest meetings with him I told him I could no longer shake his hand, as we usually did. I think he understood just how attached to him I had become. He gave me the name of a social worker and told me I could call upon her for help any time I couldn't reach him. She came out to my house once and went to great lengths to help me see that I could love my counselor without feeling guilty. I didn't realize at the time just what she was trying to tell me, but know now that she was referring to my crush on Dr. Gregory. He had been so terribly kind and understanding that I had developed quite a case on him. In fact the last time that I went to see him, I was so emotional I decided I couldn't drive home in my condition and sat in the hospital lobby for quite some time, even though the hospital had closed. Finally a policeman came over and inquired what I was doing in the lobby at that hour. I talked with the policeman for a long time, explaining to him my feelings. After talking for about half an hour, he asked if he could take me home and leave my car there for Joe who could pick it up. I told him I felt much better and would now be able to drive myself.

At the next appointment with Dr. Gregory, he told me he had helped me about as much as he could, and that he wanted me to come with Joe from that time on. He said we could either come together or take turns. I couldn't quite believe that our talks were over. I would no longer see him alone. I can't explain how I felt at the time, but the following week was the week I ended up in the hospital.

I went to St. Gabriel's Hospital the following morning with Joe. We first met with Dr. Jeffrey before going up to the floor. He told me that from what Joe had told him, he believed my problem stemmed from the decision of Dr. Gregory to cut down on my sessions. Until he told me this, I was completely unaware of the cause for my behaviors but immediately realized that this was what brought me once more to a hospital. Dr. Jeffrey told me at this time that he would put me in the open ward, and that if I would act as a mature person, he would treat me as one. I felt that he had thrown out a challenge to me, and was at once determined to meet this challenge.

Dr. Jeffrey also told Joe that he was going to put some meat on my bones. At this time I weighted 105 pounds. He gave specific orders to the dieticians about the food I should eat.

We then went to the 7th floor, which everyone knew to be the mental health ward, and Joe walked with me to my room. On the way, we passed the kitchen and I complained to Joe that I was getting sick from the smell of food coming from the kitchen. We discovered that although it was a kitchen, no food was being prepared or even standing out. It had to be my imagination that I smelled strange foods. I learned later on that I had a problem with hallucinating in smell.

That very first day I decided that I would not let my appearance and cleanliness become slovenly. The first question I asked of the nurse's aide who was assigned to me was where I could wash my hair. I was aware that it needed washing and had this on my mind until I could get it washed and set. I found a little used hair dryer and that first day I had my hair washed and set. This was to be the norm of my hospital stay. I was very bath conscious and scrupulous about keeping my clothes washed and neat. I was determined not to slip into that state of depression where one is totally oblivious of one's physical well-being.

I was conscious of one other mistake I had made during my previous hospital stays. I had always listened to others' problems and stories, trying to be a doctor myself by listening and analyzing. This time I decided to remain aloof from the other patients. This wasn't so easy to do, as I was transferred to the dormitory as soon as there was an opening. In the dormitory everyone shared everyone else's problems and of course, wanted to know mine.

I listened to the other patients trying to counsel one another and decided to tune them out. One of the patients in the dormitory had her own unique way of tuning everyone else out. She slept throughout the day and managed to keep out the noise by wearing earplugs. She would have slept through meals if they had allowed her to. Her husband came to eat lunch with her every day. She seemed very normal and lovable at these times, but immediately upon returning to her room she would once again escape to sleep and stayed that way throughout the days and nights.

This behavior aroused my curiosity, as I had never before observed anyone doing this. I realized she must have some awful memories to want to so desperately shut out the world.

One day she sat up and started talking to me. She told me of her reason for trying to sleep. She had punctured her womb trying to abort a baby she didn't want. She almost died of hemorrhaging the first time she did it. She was then allowed to go home and was once more brought by an ambulance to the hospital due to repeated hemorrhaging. She had been practicing birth control by using an IUD and had somehow become pregnant. She performed the abortion with a knitting needle.

This poor girl evidently couldn't face the horror of what she had done, as she was a very conscientious Catholic. Her husband talked with Joe quite frequently and told us that he had tried to take her out of the hospital for rides but that she tried to kill herself by jumping out of the car while on the freeway. He had to grab her and hold onto her while driving. One could see the suffering the spouses had to go through.

The lady who slept in the bed across from me was an older

woman. One day she sat and told us her story. Her oldest daughter attempted suicide and the knowledge of this had caused her to get sick herself. After she had told me this I lay on my bed and sobbed. I was relating to myself the incident of my own attempted suicide and its' damage to the ones I loved. After I got to know the other two patients and their problems, I figured it was time for me to get out of there. I felt that I was being molded into the kind of patient they had become and I didn't want to have any part of it. I told my doctor how I felt, so he had me transferred to a semi-private room.

I felt so guilty about the transfer that I couldn't get it off my mind. I was sure they regarded me as a traitor, and the more I thought about it the more ill at ease I became. Finally I decided to see who had taken my place. I saw her dresser full of statues of all kinds, rosaries and crucifixes, and then I saw the girl, about 16 years old, walk down the hall. She made such a "clumpy" noise, I couldn't believe it. I thought, "Oh, those poor women, look what they have to put up with." The girl was rather heavy and extremely odd. She had smiles for everyone, as if she thought the whole world loved her. I decided then and there to return to the dormitory. I believed that they wouldn't then suffer from my replacement. I never expected to discover the reaction of the dorm patients. They adopted this new girl, just as they had adopted me, accepting her behavior and treating her with the same love and kindness with which they had treated me. It was a good lesson in humility for me, to be equated with this strange new girl, who was so obviously sick. It made me realize that I, too, was actually sick and maybe seemed as strange to other people as this girl seemed to me.

I began to wonder if I seemed strange to the 16- year-old girl who was my new roommate. I asked her how she liked her old roommate. I was given a rather cold answer, realizing suddenly that this girl would have much rather had the young girl than this older married woman such as me. I realized not only did she not like me, but she was afraid of me.

I wondered what behavior I had performed to make her feel so hostile towards me. Later on I learned from my doctor how she probably felt. I realized I had been completely unsympathetic to the fact that she also had severe problems and needed understanding just like I did. When I began to understand this, I came to appreciate her reaction towards me. I hadn't grasped the fact that I was sick too and probably acted strange in others' eyes, just as some of the others seemed strange to me. I began to consider her feelings and kept my curtain shut most of the time.

When I had grasped the totality of the situation, I began to feel self-conscious about the fact that I was hearing strange things on my radio. Whenever I turned the radio on, no matter which station I tuned in to I always heard violin music. Everyone knows there isn't violin music on every station. I realized something was wrong and told my doctor about it. It's funny the forms mental illness takes. For me, it affected my hearing just as it had once affected my seeing. I began to panic about turning on the radio, so decided to take no chances of my roommate guessing the problem. From then on I didn't listen to the radio.

We had one other little problem to settle. She was a very popular young girl with more problems than she could cope with from her family. She had had to do all the cooking, cleaning and baby-sitting for a family of eight. She was the oldest. She had run away from home several times until her parents couldn't deal with her anymore so they had her hospitalized to be treated for emotional problems. She actually turned out to be a very sweet, conscientious young lady. Her friends visited her at night, however, and my desire was always to retire early. Whenever I was in a hospital I had a terrible time falling asleep. I got up one night and started arguing with her over her rudeness in making so much noise at my bedtime.

When the nurses reported our argument to Dr. Jeffrey, he ended up talking with me about the situation and he thought I could be more considerate. I believe that was the first time I had reacted negatively to someone else's problems. When I realized just how heartless I was to this girl, I resolved to try and make up for it by becoming the kind of roommate I should have been in the first place. Eventually, we became quite good friends but only very slowly and with much effort on both our parts. As I improved and became more compatible with the world, I also realized that she was, and always had been, much healthier than me. In fact, she had no real mental problems at all. Her problem was her family, and here she was trying to assert herself as a person worthy of a little kindness and unselfishness. I really hated to see her leave when she finally did go home.

The days at St. Michael's, with Dr. Jeffrey as my doctor, went by rather quickly. I wasn't sick enough to warrant a bodyguard. I was left pretty much on my own, given a pass whenever I wanted to do things like visit the variety store, go for early breakfast, or go to the art room.

The mornings were very busy. First of all we weighed ourselves. I never gained a pound while I was there, despite the fact that I was on a 4,000 calorie diet, eating four or five desserts a meal, drinking milkshakes mid-morning and mid-afternoon, and eating candy from the candy machine. We exercised about a half hour every morning, and the nurses said they envied my thinness and the agility I had achieved through the practice of yoga.

Each morning we were allowed to go to the art room after we had seen our doctor. This was a good reason for me to be first in line to sit in the hall outside the doctor's office. It was like waiting for confession. We were all pretty anxious to see our doctor because then we felt assured we were being treated.

I had the frame of mind that all doctors were on the sexy side. I interpreted even Dr. Jeffrey's foot touching mine as being attached to his secret desire to touch me. I was sure he enjoyed frightening me by his smile, which I also interpreted as sexy. I told this to other patients, and I'm sure some of the patients must have told him about this. Now I realize that this was only in my mind and that with his knowledge of me and my past illnesses, he most assuredly was beyond reproof in this realm. He realized just how easily I had crushes on doctors and did everything in his power to prevent this from happening with him. Then he would most certainly be unable to help me.

He made me aware of the fact that Dr. Gregory was very wrong to have been so kind and good to me. He said he lacked the professionalism in this area and convinced me that Dr. Gregory should have charged me for his sessions. He made me understand that my bad crush was the doctor's fault, and that he made a grave mistake which led me to the emotional state I was in.

I realized this with sudden impact. I wanted to call Dr. Gregory and tell him where I was. I decided to do this without notifying Dr. Jeffrey. I managed to get him on the phone and told him where I was. He said, "I'm so sorry". That's all I heard and suddenly felt I had to hang up because I couldn't even stand to hear his voice, I was so in love. That phrase rang in my mind over and over again. It became necessary for me to finally tell Dr. Jeffrey of the phone call. He simply shook his head as if he knew just how I felt. I realized from then on that I had better forget Dr. Gregory if I was ever going to recover.

Once more I was tempted to reach Dr. Gregory. I was told he would call back as soon as possible. In the meantime, I panicked and told the floor nurse about it. When the phone rang she answered it for me and told him I was busy. I never contacted him again.

One thing a mental patient must learn is how to get along with other patients, or the hospital stay could prove to be very upsetting. I discovered this at St. Gabriel's. There was a woman patient on my floor who liked to write on the blackboard that was sitting around. What she wrote, however, was usually very disturbing to me. She had been an English teacher, like I was, and was always quoting some famous author. They were usually frightening and pessimistic quotes. I, on the other hand, wanted to inspire with my writings rather than to frighten or upset. So I would turn the blackboard around and write something very inspiring on the other side. When I would leave the room, she would turn the board around to reveal her side. Rather than cause a fight, I decided to be fair and placed the blackboard horizontally so that rather than be read from one side or the other, nothing showed at all. It was my form of a truce, and the other patient respected this. She left not too long after that so I had the blackboard all to myself.

I was feeling pretty good and every morning upon rising I would walk out to the porch room, shut the door and put an inspirational record on the record player. Gradually as the other patients arose they would filter into "my" room, sit down and enjoy the music with me. When it came around to medicine time, the other patients would exclaim in amazement at the number of pills I had to take, probably because I didn't seem very ill.

One of the first friendships occurred with a man who was not even an emotionally ill patient. They had to put some "regular" patients on our floor because the hospital was overcrowded. One of these was a man who sat at the end of the hall every day. I approached him during one of my walks and as he looked very kind, I sat down and chatted with him here and there. He was an older man, all alone in the world, and seemed to enjoy my company. When it was time for him to leave, he gave me his flower display to place in the recreation room for all to enjoy.

It wasn't long before I was allowed to go to the Occupational Therapy room in the basement. I would wander around looking at all the displays, never quite able to make up my mind what to do. After a few days of this indecision, I picked up a piece of leather and decided to burn into it a saying of some sort. It was very painstaking work, for I had to print the letters in exactly the same size and fit them according to a pattern. I didn't get very far before I decided not to finish it, since it just didn't thrill me. It was then that the OT therapist helped me choose a project. I started doing some painting with acrylics which I had never before used. I wasn't doing too well so the OT lady talked me into making an oil painting instead. Once I got started, and the picture really began to look like something, I couldn't wait to come back and finish it. We were allowed to go to the art room whenever we were finished with our daily conference with our doctor and again in the afternoon when there was nothing else going on.

At once, my painting drew attention, and the OT lady, Ida Mae, took charge of me. After I had finished the first painting, the OT lady talked me into another and another, until I was finally excited about OT. I would always go down before my session with Dr. Jeffrey and always had to be called back up. Dr. Jeffrey didn't like this so he made me stay upstairs until he was finished with me. The OT lady didn't like this because now that she knew I was talented, she couldn't leave me alone. In fact, she told me that I was 100 times more talented than anyone there and that it was my duty to develop it. It was her influence that causes me to paint to this day. She made me realize that I have a gift and that I should share it with others.

Once, I told her I had done some things at home and asked if she would like to see them. She went wild when she saw the work I had done. She asked me for permission to take some pictures of my work. She begged me to leave my work done there at St. Michael's where she put them on display in different nooks and corners of the room. I was overjoyed at her enthusiasm.

I haven't said much about my problems while in the hospital. Actually, my problems developed from my fears, which were always abundant when my nerves were unruly. I developed a fear of elevators to such a degree that I wouldn't ride on an elevator with any more than one or two other people on it. I would get on the elevator and before I knew it 10 or 12 more people would get on. I'd suddenly scream that I had to get off and I'd walk into another empty elevator and go down myself. Sometimes I would be trapped into staying on the elevator when it was more than crowded. The other patients would look at me sympathetically, knowing how much I hated to be on a crowded elevator.

Another of my fears was of any test that I was required to take. I had an immensely terrific fear of taking tests. I cannot say why this was. I was scheduled to take an EEG, as all the patients were obliged to do. They told me there was nothing to it and that all you did was lay down and go to sleep. I was suspicious that there was more to it than that, and so went to take my test with much fear and trepidation. The first time I took it, it wasn't too bad. What really hit me was the fact that they wanted me to take the test over again. I immediately saw this as some dread monster about to envelop me in its awesome arms. I can't explain my fear but only remember how really terribly afraid I was. I needed comfort from the hospital chaplain. He and my husband talked to me for hours, trying to dispel my fears. The priest kindly offered to come and visit with me any time that night. In preparation for the test the patient was not allowed to sleep. I had so many fears that night that it was necessary for me to call the chaplain to come down and counsel me. He helped me get through the night.

The next morning one would think I was going to a prison, the way I acted. When I was told to do whatever they told me to do, I rebelled. I had a horrible nightmare that someone was choking me to death, and right in the middle of the test when the voice tells you not to move, I broke away from the influence of my mind, gave in to my feelings and threw the blanket off onto the floor.

After the test was completed I thought they would be upset. Instead, the nurse thanked me and told me it was a very successful test and that I wouldn't have to take it again. What they learned from that test must have been very revealing. From that day on I couldn't wear a turtleneck shirt, because it recreated that sensation of being choked that I had had during the test.

I waited by the elevator to go back to the floor, and when it opened I saw Dr. Jeffrey standing there. He suddenly looked monstrous and evil. I took one look at him and rushed out of the elevator as if I had just seen a ghost. I waited for the next elevator and awkwardly made it back to my room. I lay down on my bed and shivered in horror for a long time. I cannot explain why I was so afraid and why I dreaded that test so terribly.

I was to take yet another test. This was a brain scan, which, although much more interesting, didn't provoke the fear in me which the other test had. From the brain scan, they found that I have a slight amount of brain damage.

One of the patients I associated with was a woman with the same name and about the same weight as me only shorter. One night I was walking down the hall when I spotted her in the kitchen sobbing quietly. I walked up to her and tried to offer my sympathy. She told me she had just run away. She said that when she got out of the hospital and started running, she couldn't think of any place to run to. She cried that it was pretty bad to find out that the only place one had to run to was the mental hospital. I proceeded to tell one of the nurses on duty about Diane and that I thought she needed help.

One other time Diane was talking to me about her doctor and the fact that he was always trying to get her to tell him about herself. I convinced her that no matter how hard it was and how badly she felt about it, he should know the truth. I encouraged her to write her story and take it to him. I learned from her that she thought Jesus Christ was her father. She had seen her father, while just a young girl, hanging from the ceiling after having committed suicide. Her younger brother was forced to help her mother get him down while she stood and watched. Her husband had been seeing a psychiatrist for a couple of years, and now this was her doctor.

They had hospitalized her when she tried to drink herself to death. It was finally decided that she was the one who should be seeing a psychiatrist rather than her husband. This poor woman tried to commit suicide by drinking a bottle of shoe polish. She had to try the only way that was available. She had a wonderful personality and no one would have guessed how sick she was as she was always talking and smiling on the outside, looking as though she didn't have a problem in the world.

Before long, I was given a pass to go outside the hospital and take walks alone. One day I decided to walk to a bar that was about 10 blocks away. When I walked into the bar, I noticed that the counter was filled with men and I was the only woman. Upon looking up, I saw two huge "boobs" staring down at me and they were all lit up. That was enough for me. I turned around and left the bar immediately. I thought to myself, "What has become of me?" After that, I decided that I would never walk into a bar again. I gave up drinking altogether. Actually, I hadn't been drinking for long, but it had become a problem for me. Soon after this incident I was discharged from the hospital.

HUBERTUS, Wisconsin

"God has put something noble and good into every heart His hand created." Mark Twain

Six years passed since that last hospitalization. How did it happen? At first I struggled. Each day presented another battle. I was seeing my psychiatrist about once a week and I took the prescribed medication. Eventually the doctor visits were cut off completely, but the medication was still necessary.

This meant that I had to see someone from the hospital to keep in touch so they could prescribe my medicine. For years I talked with a social worker, nurse or counselor once every three months for a half hour. What was more essential than anything else was that I take all the medication prescribed. I was taking nine pills a day.

I felt how everybody usually feels about taking tranquilizers and anti-depressants. I was weak and was relying on pills to get me through the day. As I felt this way, I began to fight with myself to refuse the medication. I finally talked my doctor into lessening the prescription. The first result of this was an immediate retreat into suicidal tendencies. I overdosed. I remember nothing about the incident. Somehow my husband learned of it and came home immediately. He called the doctor who told him to get me dressed and bring me right to the office. How he did this and what happened when we got there I will never know. I do know that the necessity of my medication was proven by this incident. My husband was given charge of the medicine and kept it hidden from me. As much as I hated taking pills, I saw the need for them. Six years later, I still have not missed taking my nine pills a day.

Progress was slow but steady. I lived from day to day fearing each wakeful moment. I attempted to shorten the hurdle by going to bed early each night and staying in bed as late as possible in the morning. During the day I lay on the couch with the TV going steadily trying to somehow supervise my children's play. I managed to get up long enough to get meals, change the baby's diapers and do the most necessary tasks. I was ashamed of my laziness and worthlessness but I took it slowly, day by day, and eventually managed to come out of my depression.

While I went through this transitional period, I kept myself from suicide by contemplating hell. Whenever I would feel myself slipping, handling the medicine with fearful thoughts in mind, I would immediately think of hell. I told myself this was hell but at least this hell had an end. I nurtured the thought that my girls needed a mother. Even the kind of mother I was, was better than no mother at all.

I cannot say when I stopped being lethargic and started taking an interest in life. Anything that took my mind off myself was regarded as a step in the right direction. Gradually I began to take an interest in the girls and the world around me. I knew that I had been as low as anyone could possibly be without being actually dead. Now anything and everything was a step away from this horror.

Fear was with me from morning until night and it took more than a little courage to plod through each day. Yet each new moment was a triumph for me. These triumphant moments of survival led to moments of actual joy in living. I don't know when I finally left the fear and dread behind, and took up the small and simple pleasures. It happened very gradually.

It is a big jump between the way I felt in Germantown, shortly after my last hospital stay, and the way I felt in Hubertus. We built a new home out in the country. Life was absolutely fantastic. The next couple of years were unlike any I had ever lived. Maybe it was the new house, maybe it was being out in God's country, and maybe it was the medicine. I believe it was not any one thing but the combination of all things that led me to this paradise I now lived in.

My youngest child was now 6-years-old. The middle child was 8-years-old and the oldest was 10. They had miraculously grown into three lovely young ladies. Maybe this also had something to do with my temporary recovery. Now that they were no longer babies I had more freedom, more of a social life and was not busy every second of the day. However, this presented a problem for me too because I didn't know what to do with my leisure time. Now that there were periods of emptiness in the day I began to acquire new fears. I feared getting through each day's leisure time. I packed my days so full of jobs I wouldn't have time to think. This way of living gradually resolved itself. I looked around to see what other women did with their leisure time. I learned that women could become very creative housewives and mothers just by staying home and doing anything that appealed to them, such as cooking, baking or sewing. I started baking bread, canning, going to rummage sales, and to house parties. I even started oil painting. Each new acquaintance became a friend and opened a new avenue of interest.

I was now a new person, vital, interested and alive. Everything that I did, I did with enthusiasm. Each person I met I loved more than the last. The beauty of living finally took hold and I acted as a newborn baby, excited about everything which surrounded me as though it were the first time I had experienced it. I had never before felt so drawn towards people. I actually loved myself the way I was. I was ambitious, interested, and energetic. I regarded life as a bit of clay, something that can be formed and shaped and created into a work of art. My life was shaped around God. I realized that God had given it to me and that I owed Him something in return. Each new thing I did which helped shape my life was there for the asking and for the taking. I didn't want to miss anything.

I started reading and listening to the daily news which was

something that had been a source of fear for me. I could handle emergencies that arose and was unbelievably calm about trivial incidents which at one time would have been too much for me to handle. When the girls fought or whined, I didn't immediately tell myself that it was because I was a bad mother. Instead, I thought to myself that this behavior needed me to reinforce the good and try and eliminate the bad. I felt needed. I considered my obligations to my husband and family as of the utmost importance.

I knew I was better and hoped even in time to be more daring in accepting the challenges of living. There was so much to do with such little time for doing it. I gradually returned to God for inspiration in living my life. I started teaching religion to first graders. By so doing, I was able to see with a child's eyes the wonders of the world God gave us. I can't say I was all the way back, yet I knew that whatever way there was left to go, I would make it. I would make it all the way because I was not afraid.

CHICAGO, Illinois

"There are only two ways to live your life. One is as though nothing is a miracle. The other is as though everything is a miracle."
Albert Einstein

Then it happened. I became ill again. I woke in the middle of the night knowing what I had to do. I had to leave. I'd have to take the good car in order to be sure of getting anywhere. That would mean I'd have to be ready to go if my husband left the new car behind. I'd get my clothes together while the girls were getting ready for school, then take off immediately after they left. I lay there the rest of the night just planning. By the time morning came, I was all keyed up and raring to go.

The next morning I was happy to see that Joe left the new car at home. That meant I'd be able to use it for my trip. The only trouble was that Kari was sick and didn't want to go to school. I couldn't let that spoil my plans. When it was time, I called my best friend Lydia. I told her that Kari was sick and needed some medicine and asked if she would take her just while I went to the pharmacy. Of course she did.

In the meantime I put all of my clothes into the car. I had planned all night just what to pack and what to take along. Now I was ready. I didn't realize it at the time, but my manic brain was in high gear and racing like a motor. I didn't even know why I was doing what I was doing. At that time I hadn't been diagnosed as being bipolar but upon looking back, I can see that the signs had been clear for many weeks.

I wanted the family to know why I was leaving and what I was attempting to do. I typed up a letter and left it sitting in the typewriter. It said, "I will come back only after I've proven that I'm not ill". Then I left. After dropping Kari off, even though that seemed heartless to me, I started on my journey. I had no idea where I was going to go. As I drove along, I made plans. New York? Too far for the amount of gas money I had. California? I'm a bit afraid of what people are like in California. By the time I got to the supermarket, I had decided to go in and buy some food. Then I headed straight for Chicago.

As I drove into Chicago, I noticed "Hospital" signs all along the way. I decided that that would be the best place to aim for. I didn't know exactly why I wanted a hospital, but hospitals were familiar to me and I felt comfortable in them. I knew the staff was kind and caring for the most part and felt that this was the type of person I'd like to get me off in the right direction.

I came to Michael Reese Hospital. I asked for the chaplain and was given directions to find her at her home. The convent was a big old house. There were empty lots surrounding it and tenement houses could be seen in the distance. It was Chicago's south side, slums and all. I finally parked my car where I prayed it would be safe and gently knocked at the door. A young nun came to greet me. She asked me what I wanted and when I told her I needed to talk with the chaplain, she showed me into a parlor and asked me to wait. Finally Sister Joanne came into the room. She was an easy woman to talk with. We became friends immediately. I told her my whole story, along with the description of psychological abuse from my husband and she said she would do anything she could to help me. She was most cordial and extremely interested in my story of abuse and of having gone off all my medicine. My immediate problem was that I didn't have a place to sleep. Sister Joanne asked me how much money I had. It wasn't very much. She advised me to go to the YMCA downtown, as that would be the cheapest place for me.

After spending some time with Sister Joanne, I decided I needed some medicine. I returned to the hospital and asked for a psychiatrist. I was taken to the psychiatric ward where I spoke with a psychiatrist. He gave me a small bottle of Thorazine, enough to last about three days. He didn't charge anything for the medicine, for which I was very grateful.

I then drove downtown. Unknowingly, I parked by the YWCA, a place that didn't have rooms for overnight stays. So I walked to the YMCA, which was about eight blocks away. It was scary, walking the Chicago streets at night. There were men soliciting God knows what, but fortunately I made it safely to the YMCA. Here I felt even worse, because the only ones in the lobby were all men. They looked at me curiously. Why would a woman stay at a place like this? And the woman is alone! Doesn't she know better? Now I was mind-reading, at least believing that I could. They certainly looked me over. When I was shown my room at last, I didn't know how safe I would be.

That night as I lay there on my bed, I heard some men below singing loudly. The strains of the music curled their way up to my room. "Help me, Lord Jesus…" It was beautiful, being sung in a sorrowful sort of way. My emotions were a jumble of fear and sorrow with a touch of excitement. I knew I had to do what I was doing. There was not a question in my mind. But how could I survive without money? Luckily I had filled my trunk with food before leaving Hubertus. At least I wouldn't starve.

The next morning I awoke refreshed and ready to go. I didn't have any trouble finding my car, even though it was a good half hour walk. Then I drove to the north side of Chicago. I decided that I needed more money and figured I could sell my diamond. I wanted to know a little more about Chicago so I decided to park my car. I took the "L" downtown. When I got on the "L", there was a young woman in her early 20s sitting alone. She motioned to me to sit with her and we started talking. When she heard my story, she asked if I had a car. She then invited me to live with her if I would help her move. So later on, we both got off the "L" together and walked to my car. We drove to her old place and moved all of her things. She didn't have very much. She told me that she was part French and part Indian. Her name was Michelle.

When we moved into Michelle's new apartment, there was a lot of cleaning to do. I cleaned her bathroom without gloves and later wondered why my hands were so raw. We slept on the floor that night. Before going to sleep I asked her if she would go with me in the morning to downtown Chicago so I could sell my diamond. She agreed to it.

The next morning we were both up bright and early. I had only one thing on my mind, to try and get some money. We got on the bus and were on our way downtown. I felt dizzy and sick on the bus but felt sure that it was motion sickness for I had often gotten carsick in the past. But when we reached our destination, I got off the bus and immediately collapsed. After a bit, I came to only to see that a crowd had gathered around me. They told me that someone called an ambulance. One man found a big canvas, probably from a work site, and he wrapped it around me. People walked by staring. I must have looked a fright. A doctor came by and talked with me. He said I could come to his office with him and that it was right around the corner. I refused only because I knew the ambulance was on its' way.

It took a half hour for the ambulance to make its' way through the downtown traffic. When I got in I asked Michelle if she wanted to go home, but she wanted to come with me. She sat in the back seat of the ambulance while I sat in the front. There was a man sitting right behind me who leaned over and held my hand the whole time. They asked me where I wanted to go and I gave them the name of a hospital, not knowing anything about it or where it was. They looked rather astonished that I wanted to go there. The driver said, "Are you sure?" So I ended up in Lakeside Hospital on the south side. What I didn't realize is that there was a Lakeside Hospital on the north side which was a much nicer and better hospital. They took me to the one on the south side.

When we entered, they showed me to a chair and said I should wait there. There were about 30 people sitting in the waiting room.

Everyone was suffering acutely. I soon learned that I would have to wait my turn. I fainted a couple of times and this went unnoticed. The stench was unbelievable. Finally I went over to the counter and suddenly felt faint, so I lay down on the floor rather than fall down. I was sharply reprimanded and told to get up immediately. Then someone took me back to another waiting room and told me to lie down. While lying there, I learned that someone was being brought in with a gunshot wound. When the doctor finally got to me, he told me I would have to go home because they couldn't possibly keep me there. I decided that I must find out what was wrong and planned to go to Michael Reese Hospital. That was a very good decision. That all took place on a very cold and windy winter day. Besides feeling very ill, I had to brave the horrible weather.

When I finally reached Michael Reese Hospital, I asked for the doctor I had seen the day before. He wasn't there, but another psychiatrist took care of me. He told me that I had had Thorazine poisoning. The doctor who had given me a prescription the day before obviously had made a big mistake. I now had my answer, but I still faced the dilemma of how to get back to my apartment. The doctor asked me if I had any money and when I answered "no," he proceeded to find some cab tickets for me. He gave me as many as he could find and told me where I could find a taxi. He then walked me to the door. Soon, I was on my way.

As I waited on the corner a bus went by, and realizing I had enough change for the bus, I decided to hold onto my cab tickets for another time. I boarded the bus, checking to see if it would take me to the North side. Satisfied that this was the correct bus, I then climbed on sheepishly remembering what had happened only that morning. It seemed like a century ago. It was dark out now, so I closed my eyes. About an hour later I opened my eyes. It looked like we were back on the South side, so I checked it out with the driver. He said, "Lady, you slept right through your stop. We're back on the south side of Chicago."

Deeply upset, I said, "Well, then let me out right now."

Looking puzzled, he said, "Lady, are you sure? We're in the middle of nowhere right now."

113

"Yes, I'm sure. Let me out." So he proceeded to stop.

Once on the street, I realized that I was in quite a predicament. I was on a lonely, quiet street, with absolutely nothing in sight but a gas station and a lot of dark houses. I was on Chicago's south side, alone, at night!

Trying to calm myself, I said a few prayers under my breath. Then I looked across the street. There, at the gas station stood a yellow taxicab, just the kind I was supposed to look for. I quickly ran over and said to the driver that I needed a ride and asked him, all in one breath, if he accepted yellow cab tickets. He nodded yes and told me to wait a few minutes while he put gas in his car. All the way home I was worried, "What will he do if I don't have enough tickets?" When we finally reached what I called "home", I proceeded to pay him with my tickets. Amazingly, I had exactly the right amount!

All of this took place on one of the coldest, snowiest and windiest days that probably ever hit Chicago. As I plodded up the steps to my new apartment, I was greeted by Michelle. She wouldn't let me in until I convinced her that I wasn't going to be sick any more. Then, when I did get in, she asked me about the food insisting that I go and get it even before I take my coat off. So reluctantly, I was on my way once more through the terrible winds and snowdrifts looking for my car.

When I started carrying the three bags of groceries, I stumbled and fell. A man driving by noticed me and stopped. He offered to help me and took two of the bags. We talked along the way and I told him of my ordeal that day. He told me he was a doctor and that he understood Thorazine poisoning very well. Just before reaching the apartment, I asked him to go back to his car because I didn't want him to know where I lived. He understood.

Needless to say, when I finally arrived at my "home", we had a good meal and I went to bed exhausted immediately afterwards. For both of us the "bed" was on the floor.

The next morning I was up bright and early. Michelle slept quite late so I had to spend a few hours on my own. I went down to the "Courtyard" where all the tenants were seated. It was enjoyable talking with some of the old men and women. After that I gathered up my photo albums and visited the landlady. After sharing my pictures with her, pictures of my home and my children, I asked her if I could rent an apartment for myself. She agreed to it, much to my amazement. Of course, I promised her I was going to obtain a big amount of money, and she believed me. Looking back, I can't figure out exactly where that money was going to be coming from.

I went back to our apartment and looked up the name of a psychiatrist. Upon calling him, I made an appointment for that afternoon. You might wonder why I would call a psychiatrist, but the whole purpose of my journey was to prove that I wasn't mentally ill. For this reason, I needed a psychiatrist to attest to that fact.

I offered my diamond to Michelle as a gift of gratitude, but she wouldn't accept it. So I gave her my rabbit jacket, which Joe had bought for me. It was a very beautiful jacket and Michelle was very pleased.

In the early afternoon, I got into my car and drove downtown. I had to park in a parking structure which I hadn't planned on, for I had no money. But I decided I had to and that I would find a way of getting out. I just trusted in my ability to do almost anything.

I went to Dr. Weiss' office and answered all his questions to the best of my ability. After a time, he presented me with a piece of paper which he wanted me to sign, wherein I would be signing away my freedom if he should decide I needed hospitalization. For some reason, I hadn't counted on anything like that happening and I wasn't prepared to handle it. I just signed.

Dr. Weiss was a serious psychiatrist. I was completely unnerved by my association with him. When I left his office, I remember considering myself lucky that he didn't commit me right then and there. I'll never forget what happened next.

I was in this very large building and probably took the wrong stairs. When I got to the bottom and pushed through the door, I saw a door to my left and one to my right and ahead of me was a wall. I couldn't budge either door and I panicked. My thoughts were, "This is their trick to trap me. I'll never get out of here." I also thought,

"They want to keep me locked in here until I actually do go crazy." My heart raced and I became covered with sweat. My mind became more confused in its' panic than it had ever been in my lifetime. Finally I decided I'd have to calm myself somehow if I was going to get out of there. I thought back to Fran and Bob, the charismatics who had urged me to give up my medicine. I knew what they would say. "Whenever you're in trouble, just say the word Jesus and all will be well." So I tried it. As I said the word over and over, Jesus, Jesus, Jesus, I found myself calming down. Once I calmed down, I realized that all I had to do was to turn around and go through the same door leading up the stairs. I climbed the stairs, legs shaking, heart pounding, and looked for a different exit. Finally I found my way out of the building and through the streets to my car.

When I found my car, I realized that I had no money to get it out of the parking lot and decided I must go back to the psychiatrist and ask him for money. That was one of the hardest things I've ever had to do. He said he had a meeting to attend and that he would raise the question there. After about a half hour he came out and handed me $4. I was happy to be out of there a second time and on my way.

When I was in my car driving slowly through downtown Chicago, traffic jammed in every direction, I suddenly realized I had no money for gas. At the same time, I became frightened that they could put me in the hospital at any time because of what I had signed and the address I had given to Dr. Weiss. I decided then and there that I had to get out of Chicago and away as fast as possible. I went to the telegraph station and wired Fran and Bob asking them to send $100 to me. For some reason, I was told to go to another station to pick up the money. I had parked my car in an alley and made sure I knew the street it was on. Then I raced about eight long blocks to the other station knowing they closed at 4:30 p.m. and that I barely had time to get there. I made it just in time but Fran and Bob had not sent me any money.

Terribly disappointed, I walked hastily back to my car and wracked my brain for how to get some money. I decided to look for a church and when I did find one, I figured I'd better get into my old clothes so I'd look poor enough to beg. I couldn't change my pants in the car so carried my jeans to the church and ducked into a bathroom. I left my good white slacks in the bathroom wastebasket. A priest came out and introduced himself as Father Ronald. He talked with me for a long time. I told him my predicament and that I could be committed if they found me. He gave me $5 and told me the best way to go is to get far away from Chicago and in the opposite direction of Milwaukee. He directed me to St. Louis.

I left Chicago according to the priest's instructions, supposedly heading in the direction of St. Louis. It was night and I was tired. When I finally was able to see where I was, I saw a sign saying "Lake Geneva." I knew that that meant I was headed for the Playboy Club and I was glad, for I knew that somehow that meant I could get money. At that point I didn't know how I would get it, but I saw the possibility it promised.

Because I was so dead tired by that time, the first thing I wanted to do was to take a nap. I tried to figure out where it would be safe and decided to look for a restaurant with cars parked outside, feeling that this would be the safest place. I found one and parked my car alongside all the other cars. Then I slid down onto the seat where no one could see me and tried to sleep. Because it was in the middle of winter, I could only sleep a couple of hours before I got too cold. But that couple of hours was nice. I felt rested and ready to go on.

Since I was headed for the Playboy Club, I decided to change my clothes once again. This time I shed the ragged clothes and put on my best. I put on a deep red silk blouse and changed into a nice pair of slacks. Then I took off my old jacket and put on my dark brown suede coat with the fox fur collar. When I finally reached the Playboy Club, I drove in along the entrance road and was stopped halfway by a person in a small office. I was asked to give him my Playboy Club Card but I said I had forgotten it in my room. He allowed me to go in. As I climbed the stairs, I felt a sense of awe that I had been allowed in and I felt I'd have to look like I knew what I was about.

After looking around, I settled on going to the bar. I went in and sat down with no money. .I don't know how long they would have let me stay there, but fortunately two very nice men came along and sat down beside me. Before long I had something to drink. The men introduced themselves and asked about me. I told them that I had stopped there because I was out of money and needed $10 for gas. Then I told them my story. They were very good listeners, but every so often one of them would ask, "You're not a hooker? Are you sure you're not a hooker?"

I noticed a young couple sitting way across the bar nudge each other, look at me and grin. I knew what they were thinking. But I kept assuring the two men that I was not a hooker. They wanted to know what I planned to do that evening. I said I was going to sleep in my car. They were stunned. They couldn't believe that I would even think of it, seeing how cold and unsafe it was. I told them that I didn't have any choice. The younger man kept asking me to sleep in his room for the night. I stated no again and again. I just couldn't. They consulted with each other and told me that they wouldn't allow me to sleep in my car. They were going to pay for a room for me for that night...a room of my own. They also gave me money for gas.

While we talked that night, the men also talked about themselves. The older man had had a daughter killed in a car accident a few years earlier. I figured he was kind to me because, in a way, I probably reminded him of his daughter.

What these two men actually did was to pay for a room for me for $80. That night, when I went into this beautiful room, I could hardly believe my eyes. I turned the TV on, but because I had missed so much sleep, my mind was not working well and I couldn't make sense out of the TV. Instead, I sat down at the desk and wrote a letter of thanks to the two men. I was so grateful that I made a decision which they had encouraged me to do. In the letter I told them to wait for me in the morning. I was going to call my husband, as they had urged me to do, and I would have him give me the money to reimburse them. I was just too overwhelmed. I thought that if they could be so good to me, then I should do something for them. I was going back to my husband.

When I talked with Joe that night, he told me what time I should be up and waiting for him. I asked him for the money to repay the two gentlemen, and he gave it to me. When I asked for them at the office, I was told they had left much earlier. I shall always be grateful for what those two men did for me.

Joe came with his brother, Ken. When I went out, I was very concerned that the car should look nice, so I went out to wipe it down before Joe would see it. As I was going over the car, Ken saw me and came over. I'll never forget how he looked at me. It's hard to describe, but I think he thought he was looking at a crazy woman and a floozy combined. I was neither. I was fine. When I saw Joe a little later, I had the definite feeling that he was happier to get his car back than he was to have me back. All the way home he talked about how sick I was. It was not a very enjoyable homecoming.

RACINE, Wisconsin

"You can't multiply happiness by dividing it." Anonymous

I arrived home but I wasn't to be there for long. I hardly had time to say hello to my girls, when my husband called a hospital and had me admitted. When I walked down the halls of Milwaukee Catholic Hospital, I laughed and joked and talked with everyone. I couldn't have been happier. The truth is, I was very manic.

Before long, the doctor gave me so much medicine I couldn't even get out of bed. I was hopelessly depressed. My mother and father visited me at that time. My father started yelling at me and told me to get out of bed, that there was nothing wrong with me. The nurse had to usher my father out of the room. That was the second time my father had to be ushered out of my hospital room.

I was soon to learn that Dr. Vin ordered me to have shock treatments. Upon hearing this, I went to talk with the Chaplain, Father Bill. We had talked previously, and he felt that Dr. Vin was making a terrible mistake. He advised me to get out of the hospital any way I could. He arranged for someone from Sojourner Truth House to pick me up, if I did manage to escape. When I left the hospital, I was supposed to call them and someone would come and get me.

I went to my room, packed my bags and gave my beautiful gift of artificial flowers to my roommate. I put on my coat and walked past the desk. I stood there with my back to the desk, as though I was a visitor, and as soon as the door opened I walked out. I just kept walking until I was outside. Once I was away from the hospital, I looked for a place where I could make the phone call. The only place I could see was a tavern, so I went in only to discover that I didn't have a quarter. I told the bartender I'd give him my watch for a quarter, and he, seeing how desperate I was, gave me a quarter and told me to keep my watch. The trouble was, when I called the number Father Bill had given me, they didn't have a car available. I knew I couldn't wait around there for long because they'd be looking for me, so I rushed out and walked up to Wisconsin Avenue where I flagged down a taxi. A woman was driving and I told her I didn't have any money but that if she'd take me to the bank, I'd pay her. It was fortunate that it was a woman driver, for she was very compassionate. She drove me to the bank and I paid her generously. I then asked her to take me to Racine, where I was to go to a women's shelter.

Upon arriving in Racine, I took the taxi driver out to eat. When I arrived at the shelter, Phyllis, the head counselor, welcomed me and showed me where I would be sleeping. It looked like very cramped quarters, but I felt lucky to be there.

That night, I discovered that I had a Boston Store charge card in my purse, so the next morning I took the bus back to Milwaukee and went on a shopping spree. I started on the ground floor and worked my way up. On each floor, I bought whatever appealed to me. I bought a blanket and comforter for my new bed in the shelter. I bought an outfit for the little 5-year-old boy who lived in the shelter. I bought a couple of new outfits for myself. When I reached the top floor, I had two bundles as tall as I was. One of the store clerks questioned my integrity and they checked me out. Everything was OK, so I departed for the bus depot with my purchases.

Phyllis decided that I should go off of all my medication. I was easy to persuade because I never did accept the fact that I needed so much medication. Actually, I didn't think I needed any medicine, as

I didn't consider myself mentally ill. For that reason, I decided to see a psychologist in Milwaukee to prove that I wasn't mentally ill. I took the bus back to Milwaukee again. When I met with the psychologist and took all his tests, it became clear to me that I did have a tremendous mental problem and that I was mentally ill after all. This caused me to become so distraught that that night, when I returned on the bus, I decided to go out and get drunk.

I went to a nearby bar and just kept ordering drink after drink. Pretty soon I fell off the bar stool and the bartender called the police. They put me on a stretcher and took me to the hospital. At the hospital they asked who I could call to come and pick me us, so I gave them Phyllis' name at the women's shelter. She came to get me, but she was intensely angry. She told me that this was the one and only time she would rescue me, and that for the future I should find another rescuer.

Phyllis would not let me go out of the shelter any longer, for she said my husband had detectives out looking for me. After being cooped up in the women's shelter for weeks, I was going crazy and decided I had to take a walk. I put on tons of makeup, knowing that they were looking for a woman who wore very little makeup. I walked so far that day that Phyllis couldn't believe it. After that, I took a long walk every day.

It was very difficult to go off my medication. The withdrawal symptoms were horrible. I couldn't sleep at night and didn't know what to do with myself. Nights were very bad. Sometimes I would call people I knew, like Father Bill, in the middle of the night, and they would get very angry with me.

Phyllis was worried that the detectives would find me, so she decided to send me to a shelter in Saginaw, MI. In the process, she had a psychologist test me to see how sick I really was. She had it all set up. One night I had to sleep at a motel and in the morning I was supposed to board a plane which would fly me to Saginaw. However, that very day she received the scores from my test. Evidently, they discovered that I was quite sane and for that reason decided to cancel the flight.

Time passed swiftly. Before long, I managed to get a job and rent my own apartment. I was still going out to bars at night alone. Coming home one night from a bar, I walked into my apartment. I saw several liquor bottles on the kitchen table. Becoming totally confused because I had never bought any liquor, I suddenly realized this couldn't be my kitchen. I was in the wrong apartment.

My usual evenings were spent in bars. One night I went to a bar and a man started buying me drinks. After a time, he looked at me and said, "I'm cutting you off. You've had enough to drink." Then he asked me if he could drive me home. The bartender told me to beware of this man, that his wife had just committed suicide. Realizing that the bartender was trying to warn me, I went with the man anyway. However, I had a feeling deep in my gut that something was not right. While driving, the man kept asking for my address. It came to me that I shouldn't tell him, that I didn't want him to know where I lived. He became very insistent, but the more he insisted, the more I sensed danger.

Suddenly I jumped out of the car. He stopped and ran after me and shoved me back into the car. Then he started driving again. Once more I jumped out of the car and this time I ran with all my might. Fortunately, I spotted the YMCA ahead of me and made a wild dash to it's' front door. Once inside, I knew I was safe. It was late and there weren't many people there, so I just lay down on a bench and slept through the night. In the morning, when they discovered me, they scolded me harshly for sleeping there. I didn't care. I was safe and that was all that mattered. I walked back to my apartment in wonderment at my narrow escape.

By this time, the men I met in bars knew I was an easy target and I ended up taking a few men home with me. It became clear to my counselor that I wasn't doing well on my own, so she decided I needed to come back to the shelter. However, the shelter was so full, she decided to get a hotel room for me. This was not a good idea, for there was a bar at this hotel and a floor show. Being very manic, I decided to have a party in my room. The next day, I made several trips to the library and checked out many beautiful paintings with which I decorated my room. I also made several trips to the downtown stores. By the time I was finished, my room looked very beautiful.

Because I was so frantically manic, instead of having the party I decided to admit myself to the mental hospital at St. Lukes. Once I was admitted, I simply continued my process of decorating. I took down all the pictures that I saw in the halls and took them to my room. Before long, my room looked lovely. I was so proud of myself, in my mania, that I invited other patients into my room to see how I had decorated it.

I wasn't able to enjoy myself for long, because Dr. Paul came in and told me that he was committing me and that I had to go to a locked ward. I was furious! I was so manic by that time that nothing could stop me. For some reason, I had a dime and hid it under my tongue. When I found myself locked in the room, I took the dime out of my mouth and proceeded to unscrew everything that I could. Later on when the aid came in and tried to turn on the light, he received a shock. He was very angry with me. There was another patient in the room, but he became so frightened of me they had to move him out.

The entire time I was in that room I carried on with extreme mania. I had brought several magazines along with me from the other room. There was a bottle of hand lotion in the bathroom. I tore out words and pictures to send messages to my doctor. I smeared these with hand lotion and stuck them to the window. I repeated message after message in this way. My mania was so severe that they finally came in and strapped my hands and feet to the bed. I managed to work the mattress off the bed, so they just left me like that. After lying there for a long time, a public defendant came and talked with me. By that time, I had calmed down considerably. The lawyer looked at me with compassion and said, "In the future, you may look back and forgive them for what they have done to you." After talking with the lawyer in a very sane way, he somehow got me out of being committed and I was free to go home. I showered and dressed in one of my new outfits. I looked like a million dollars. While talking with the nurse's aides who were men, I invited them to my party at the hotel. Believe it or not, they came to my party that night.

Back at the hotel, there was a floor show going on. I went to my hotel room and dressed in my nicest dress. Instead of wearing the rope belt around my waist, I tied it around my head. This gave me a rather "hippy" look. I then walked down to the floor show. Walking right up to the MC, I asked him if I could sing. I sang three songs and the audience loved me. Upon leaving the stage, I invited everyone to my party saying that it was in celebration of winning the commitment. Later on a man came by and gave me a bottle of brandy. I ran cold water in the bathtub to cool it off. And then my party began.

I had a wonderful party that night. In the morning I realized I had slept with one of the aides from the hospital. He made me promise that I wouldn't call him at the hospital. I knew that if I called him I'd get him into deep trouble. I didn't want to do that to him. That morning I realized how out of control I was. I decided to clean up the room. I took all the pictures back to the library, put my bed back together, cleaned the room, packed my bags and decided to give everything away. I left my suitcases sitting in the hallway for anyone to take. Later on the people from the shelter came and gathered my bags.

At this time, my only concern was to get myself to a hospital. Calling Dr. Dick in Milwaukee, I told him that I needed to go to a hospital. He told me that he knew of a very special hospital, where they would respect me and that it was suited to my special needs. This was Richard's Hospital in Oconomowoc. My only concern was, how was I going to get to Oconomowoc? While conversing with Dr. Dick, I noticed a man sitting nearby who was listening to the whole conversation. Afterwards, he came up to me and asked if I needed a ride. He offered to take me to Oconomowoc and I accepted. I felt I wasn't in any position to refuse, as I could think of no other way to get from Racine to Oconomowoc.

As we were driving along, I noticed that he started slowing down. He told me he didn't think I was very ill. I became very frightened. I decided that maybe if I acted ill he would forget his bad intentions. I slipped down onto the floor just like a mental patient would do. From then on, he drove in earnest until we arrived at Richard's Hospital.

OCONOMOWOC, Wisconsin

"Forget not that the earth delights to feel your bare feet and the winds long to play in your hair." Kahlil Gibran

Upon arriving at Richard's Hospital, we were greeted by a couple of nurses. They couldn't get me to budge from my perch on the car floor. They softly persuaded me, and I finally got out. They took me to my room and left me alone. I shut the door and proceeded with the many preparations to make this into my "personal" room. I completely dismantled the bed. I took down the drapes and put up the bedspread for drapes. I used the drapes to cover what was no longer a bed. I balanced the ends of the bed against the wall to make them look like shelves. By the time the nurse came back, my room was in total disarray. She stared in disbelief and went running to get her supervisor.

When the nursing supervisor came in, she told me in no uncertain terms that it just wouldn't do. She said that everything was too dangerous. They then took me to another room with orders to leave it intact, although they were very nice about it and explained that they were mainly concerned for my safety. During my stay at Richard's Hospital, Dr. Dick drove out from Milwaukee twice a week to see me. He was very solicitous for my improvement and proved to be a very caring doctor. After I had been there only a week, Dr. Dick decided I had improved greatly. He told me he was going to pay for a room for me in a hotel in Milwaukee. This sounded strange to me, but I realized that Joe wouldn't want me at home.

The first night at the hotel I walked down to the bar and a man started buying drinks for me. Before I knew it, this strange man came into my room. Just then the phone rang. It was Dr. Dick. He asked, "Is there a man in your room?" I answered yes and he demanded I give the phone to the man. I could hear him yell to the frightened man, "Get the hell out of there!" The man left immediately.

The following night I went to the bar again. The bartender came over to me and said, "I have orders that I cannot serve you any drinks." I said, "I'll show you!" I went up to my room and got the medicine bottle, took it down to the bar and started swallowing all the pills. No one said anything to me, so I returned to my room. I began thinking about what I had done and fearful of brain damage, decided I'd better call Dr. Dick. He told me to sleep it off, because it wasn't enough medicine to hurt me. Not believing him, I called the police. The police came soon and took me to Mt. Sinai Hospital, where they pumped my stomach. Upon leaving Mt. Sinai I didn't know what to do, so I walked to Jesu Church and talked with a priest. He counseled me to go back to the hospital where I had been a patient, in other words, Richard's Hospital. When I returned to my hotel room, I once again called Dr. Dick, and before long I found myself back at Richard's Hospital. This was the beginning of a long stay.

In the earlier months of my stay at Richard's , I learned that I could leave the premises and walk to the Olympia, which was a nightclub two miles away. Another woman usually went with me. Three different times I went and three different men took me to bed. One of the men I slept with told me he had just admitted his wife to a mental hospital. Sure enough, the next day I met his wife who was a patient on my floor. That was the last straw for me and it put an end to my escapades.

After some time at Richard's Hospital, Dr. Dick decided once again that I was well enough to go home. This time, he did succeed in getting Joe to take me home. But he was mistaken once again because in just a few days, Joe returned me to the hospital. While Joe was in the process of admitting me, we walked into the gift shop as a family. I started buying very expensive gifts for all of the girls using my charge card. The lady in the gift shop didn't know that I was a patient. I felt sorry for the girls because when Joe returned and saw what I had done, he made the girls return their gifts.

At this time I was extremely manic. I promised the girls that I was going to build on to the hospital for them. I would build a horse ranch and would buy each of them a horse. Unfortunately, Anne Marie, my youngest, believed everything I told her. I think the older girls were onto me.

For quite a while, I was in a heightened manic state. I never slept more than two hours at night. Each night I was out in the dayroom with all the staff instead of in my bed. I couldn't sleep. This is very typical of people in the manic state.

One night I decided I wanted to take a walk. This was at about 2 a.m. Of course, they weren't about to allow me to walk at that hour. Besides, it was raining heavily. I walked around checking all the windows to see how I could get out. I finally found an open window which led out onto a porch roof. I walked out onto the roof and threatened to jump if they didn't let me walk in the rain.

The staff called Dr. Dick and he told them to let me take the walk. I came in off the porch, put on my poncho and as I went out the front door, I grabbed the wastebasket liner which I used as a raincoat. I walked and walked and some very strange occurrences took place in my head. I was sure that I was pregnant because of the men I had been to bed with, and that I was going to be the mother of Jesus. I tried to figure, using age calculations, which man would be the father of my child. I was on my way to the president of the United States to tell him the news about being the mother of Jesus.

While walking, I became rather warm and had to shed some of my clothing. Later on the police would find this clothing and assume that I was raped. As I walked on for about 2 or 3 miles, my ideas about Jesus and the president dwindled to nothing and I decided to turn back.

A police car drove up behind me and they took me back to the hospital. When we approached the hospital, what a sight met my eyes. There were about five police cars there and Dr. Dick was standing on the steps shouting. It seems they wanted to send me to Winnebago, a hospital for the more seriously ill, but he insisted that I wasn't bad enough and that they should let me remain at Richard's. He won.

That night seemed to be the breaking point—the point where I broke out of my illness. From then on I began to improve. I started taking long walks around the lake. These were five mile walks which I took every day. In the beginning I thought a lot about suicide, but gradually even those thoughts left me. I know that I meditated a great deal on those walks. Nature was so beautifully rich and engulfed me in its' arms. I was alone with nature, alone with my God. Over a period of time I began to heal.

Finally I was well. I had been in the hospital eight months. Dr. Dick wanted me to go home but Joe wouldn't come and get me. One day Dr. Dick told me I was the only patient he'd ever had who was well and had no one to come and take out of the hospital. Everyone knew I was well. They were as anxious for me to leave as I was.

MILWAUKEE, Wisconsin

"It is difficult to say what is impossible, for the dream of yesterday is the hope of today and the reality of tomorrow." Robert H. Goddard

One lovely, sun-filled fall afternoon, I packed my bags and walked a couple of miles to the bus stop. No one at the hospital tried to stop me. The bus took me to Milwaukee. As I walked along the streets of Milwaukee, I knew where I was headed. I knew that Casa Maria was a shelter for homeless people. Arriving there late in the afternoon, I was warmly welcomed by the staff, but they were baffled as to where they would put me because the shelter was very full. In the end, they decided I could sleep in the playroom. Early the next morning, they showed me to a room of my own on the second floor.

During the day I mingled with all the other "guests" at Casa Maria. By that time, I was feeling so well that I was encouraged to try and find a job. After just a few days, I walked to downtown Milwaukee and applied for a job at a bank. Unbelievably, they hired me. Since it was a long walk from Casa Maria, I moved into the YMCA.

I learned that Dr. Dick's office was only two blocks away from the bank where I worked so I stopped by his office. He invited me to visit him every day during the noon hour break. After I had been doing this for some time, I started worrying about how I was going to pay him. Dr. Dick simply smiled at me and told me not to worry because Joe would pay for the visits. I said, "Every day?" Dr. Dick told me to lie to him if he asked me how often I was seeing him. That sent up a danger signal for me. All my life I had a strict inner sense about lying. I wouldn't lie about anything. My motto was, "I wouldn't lie to save the world." Because of this, I started losing confidence in Dr. Dick and stopped visiting him.

Now that I was feeling so well, it was only natural that I spent a lot of time thinking about my girls. I longed to see them and to be with them. Every night when I went to my room in the YMCA, I would call Joe and beg him to let me come home. Each night was spent in tears for the answer was always an emphatic "no."

I never gave up trying. I called and called. Each night I came home from work, preparing myself emotionally for rejection. Then, unexpectedly, one night he said "yes." I was ecstatic! That night I couldn't sleep. I could hardly wait for morning to come when I would see my girls and be with them. I will never forget that reunion.

I must admit that my husband was being very charitable and forgiving. He knew that I had committed adultery a number of times, because I had shared this with him. He simply wanted to wait until he was sure I wasn't pregnant. God was very good to me to preserve me from this.

After being home just a short time, Joe and I were back together physically, emotionally and psychologically. I was determined that I would never again leave my family and my home. It was difficult at first to face my neighbors. I could only imagine the rumors that had spread about me. Actually, everyone treated me so well I could hardly believe it. Soon everything was back to normal.

I was in a very meditative mood. I started making two quilts for the girls' bunk beds, which took nearly a year to complete. While doing my quilting, I loved to quietly muse over the marvel that my life was so wonderful once again. Quilting for me was very comforting and therapeutic.

The next seven years went by without too much trouble. At first

I had a problem with alcohol, but before too long it was under control. My daughters saw me drunk only twice. Once when Joe and I went to a neighborhood "pig roast" and Joe had to stuff me into the car and drive me home. The girls thought I was dead, but I was only "dead drunk". Another time happened while the girls were away at school. I decided that I needed to cry and felt that drinking brandy would help. When the girls came home from school they found me in bed, but instead of crying, I was laughing hysterically. I had consumed almost the entire bottle of brandy.

Joe managed to keep control of the liquor supply. After a time of hiding liquor, I could no longer find any bottles to hide. Since I had no money and Joe never gave me any, I had no way of purchasing more liquor, so my drinking problem completely disappeared.

Those seven years went by slowly for me. I was a stay-at-home mom, for which I was very grateful. I loved to do housework and help the girls with their homework. Each afternoon found me baking a treat for the girls. When they got off the bus, they came home wondering what treat Mom had made for them that day. Time sometimes lay its' heavy hands on me but I managed to stay busy and conquered my tendency towards depression.

If it weren't for my mental illness, I may still be married today. However, as time went on I began feeling that my marriage was anything but satisfactory. I often asked Joe if we could get marriage counseling, but his answer was always the same. "You're the only one with a problem."

One day I approached Joe while he was cutting the grass. I said, "I want a divorce." His answer was so simple, yet so final. He said, "Don't ever, ever change your mind." That was it. There was no further discussion. From that time until the day I left, we never discussed it.

I left in the spring of 1985. Having no money, I felt that I had to sell my diamond ring if I had any hope of hiring a lawyer. The first two lawyers I hired were "do nothing" lawyers. I had left Joe and moved to West Bend. These male lawyers did absolutely nothing for me. I then sought a woman lawyer and found an excellent one in

Milwaukee. She did wonders for me and was very supportive. It was hard to keep in contact, for her office was on Wisconsin Avenue in Milwaukee, but I managed to drive there several times.

When I asked for the divorce, one of my daughters was in college and another soon to graduate from high school. My youngest, who was 15-years-old at the time, was the only one who bore the brunt of the divorce. The divorce hit her the hardest because she felt she was to blame. For a time, she came and lived with me in West Bend and went to the West Bend High School. When she left me and went to live with her dad, I experienced some of my most difficult times. I couldn't get used to living alone. When I'd come home from work and stare at the blank walls and empty rooms, I couldn't face being alone. Often times I'd walk to the liquor store and then go home laden with my rescuer, the liquor.

At this time I was being counseled by Robert, from the Division of Vocational Rehabilitation. My DVR counselor became aware of my drinking problem and advised me to seek help. I accepted his advice and went to outpatient rehabilitation. I became involved in the 12 step program which I'm still involved in to this very day. It saved my life. Being very impressionable, when I viewed videos about drunken driving, I became aware of the dangers of drinking. I realized that the only way I was going to succeed in my life was to quit drinking.

Life in West Bend was not easy for me. I moved several times within the first couple of years. I also held several different jobs within just a few years. One of these jobs was at Kremers-Urban Pharmaceutical Company. It was an excellent job and I had a wonderful position as secretary to the Director of Marketing. Everyone there was supportive of me in my divorce. I was open and friendly with all of my fellow employees. But then something went terribly wrong. I began thinking that someone there was going to kill me. I became so paranoid that I couldn't continue working there. Before too long, I had a full-scale nervous breakdown.

WAUWATOSA, Wisconsin III

"You can clutch the past so tightly to your chest that it leaves your arms too full to embrace the present." Jan Glidewell

It all started with my late evening walk to the police station. I told them that I wanted them to take my new car as I was going to New York to be a street person. I was playing a game with them. Before they could question me, I ran off and they proceeded to chase me. I ran over lawns and between houses as fast as I could, and they finally caught up with me. Consequently, I was taken to the Police Station where they questioned me. I heard one policeman telling the others, "We can't leave her alone. At one hospital she broke the light bulb and cut herself." Amazed by the fact they had this piece of information about me after such a short time, I became aware of the situation I had gotten myself into. Consequently, I was taken to the mental hospital in West Bend. I was there only half of the next day when I demanded to see my lawyer. I was able to contact her by phone but she wasn't able to help me. Before I knew it, I was being taken by ambulance to Mercy Hospital in Wauwatosa, WI.

As I look back, I see that there were several things going on with me at once. I was out of my head some of the time and clearheaded at other times. Much of the time I was frightened. When I was alone, I managed to sort everything out. But most of the time in the hospital

I was among other patients who were also out of their mind and frightened. On looking back, I can only remember incidents, but I can't put these incidents in any logical order.

One of the first days I was at Mercy Psychiatric Hospital, I received a picture in the mail from a missionary I knew. It was his rendition of the Compassionate Jesus, an oil painting. It greatly consoled me, for it was a reminder to me that the good Lord would be there with me through it all.

Another pleasant gift surprised me. I had made out several orders for women I worked with for beautiful gifts. They had ordered gifts to give to other people at a House Party that I had hosted. When the box of gifts arrived, I decided to pay for it all myself and give out the gifts to the other patients. This was found to be an extremely rewarding undertaking. To me it seemed almost miraculous, especially in one instance.

The woman in the room next to mine sat in the middle of her room on a chair every day, day after day. No one could get her to get off the chair and try to walk. The day after I gave her my gift she was walking up and down the hall. The nurses and aides were amazed. I felt that it was the gift that caused her to get up and walk. Upon looking back, I realize that this probably wasn't true at all.

One symptom I was bothered with while I was there was that I hallucinated in smell. I always smelled smoke. When I'd mention this to the nurse, I was told that people were probably burning wood in their fireplaces in the neighborhood.

Eventually I came to realize that the smoke smell was not real and that in my mind I had deserted my girls by leaving them behind. This image was so vivid and smothered me so that it came to the surface in another form. Of course, this is my unprofessional interpretation of my strange preoccupation with the smell of smoke. I came to realize that people wouldn't be burning wood in the summertime.

Evidently I did not have a good feeling about my psychiatrist, Dr. Steve. Dr. Steve is a very nice-looking man about my age with an air about him that tells me he has never experienced anything tragic and is incapable of empathizing with someone who has. He seems head and shoulders above pain and suffering. Therefore, anything I said to him didn't seem to penetrate very far. I didn't know I had such an aversion to him until one day when he was supposed to meet me in my room.

Subconsciously, I felt that I had to prevent him from coming into my room. I blocked the door by pushing all the furniture to the middle of the room and against the door. When he came to my room, he couldn't budge the door. I then remembered what he had told me time after time: "When you feel depressed or stressed, take a shower." So I got into the shower and turned the water on full blast. I don't remember how they finally got the door open. All I know is that he was fuming. I felt happy that I had made him angry. The other patients told me later how he had been standing in the hall screaming and swearing at me. I would have loved to hear it. Dr. Steve wasn't really the one I was angry at, but he provided a good target. There were very many ways in which he resembled my ex-husband.

Later on, the staff took some of my furniture out of the room, but once again I managed to barricade the door. I pushed everything together and when I saw that there was an empty space, I used my body to fill it. This made it even more impossible for them to get in because whenever they'd push, I'd scream in pain. This baffled them to no end. I don't remember who won the battle but I do remember, however, how these incidents changed everyone's attitude towards me. Suddenly, instead of being a pleasant patient who was reachable and touchable, I was somewhat of an enigma, both distant and paranoid. The staff was both afraid of me and perplexed by my behavior. I was changed and found myself in an unacceptable position. Only a few of the patients could get close to me. The staff no longer could.

One day I was talking with a young girl. She came to my room to see the poetry I had written. When she read my poems, she exclaimed, "If I could write poetry like that I'd be a millionaire." We then went to her room and she shared her poetry with me. Her poems were like some I'd seen before written by a schizophrenic where the important thing seemed to be the rhyming sounds.

One day I found myself struggling to get up off the floor. The aide was standing by the door screaming at me. He was getting angrier and angrier because he thought I was pretending. The truth is, I just couldn't get off the floor. Another evening, I remember being handed from one counselor to another because they couldn't "reach" me. I was momentarily tempted to lose touch with reality altogether. I never wanted to talk again. I knew that I could do it, but it was a temptation I resisted.

One of the counselors succeeded with me where all of the others failed. His name was Kurt. Kurt couldn't understand why I'd never go to the cafeteria to eat but would instead have the food brought to me on the floor. He was talking with me in my room one day and I agreed to go to the cafeteria with him to try and eat. He learned that I had been made fun of by my ex-husband while eating and that I was afraid to eat in public for fear of making mistakes and being humiliated.

Kurt was a very special person to me. He was the only one I trusted—the only counselor who seemed to think there was something in me worth saving. When he went to the cafeteria, he took me to secluded spot where I could relax. He gently coaxed me through my meal. Eventually he helped me overcome my sensitivity and I started going to the cafeteria.

For some reason, I decided to make this hospitalization a time of grieving for the death of my brother, Eddie. Eddie was one and a half years older than me, and we had always been very close both as little children and on through adulthood. Four years earlier, Eddie had committed suicide. My ex-husband and I had gone to the funeral home. At the funeral home, when my mother walked over to the side of the coffin where they had Eddie lying out for all to see, my mother "lost it". I quickly ran over to her and held her and comforted her. In doing so, my own grieving was stifled and I didn't even shed a tear. I know I grieved as much as or more than anyone, but there was no exterior release. Now here in the hospital, I figured it was a good time for it.

I used the picture of Christ that I had received in the mail. I placed the picture on the shelf in the closet. With a bouquet of flowers arranged behind the picture and my Bible set in front, I decided to place Eddie's name, date of birth and date of death inside the Bible. Somewhere I found a candle and every night after the nurse made the final room check, I'd open the closet door and sit up and gently cry for Eddie. Night after night I sat there thinking of my dead brother and crying, and no one ever knew.

I had deteriorated by now, so that they called me a medical failure and felt there wasn't anything anyone on Sleyster Hall could do for me. So they transferred me to Brooker Hall. The people on Sleyster felt that perhaps some other place, geared to the more severely ill, would be able to do something for me that they couldn't do. I was sure that the reason they moved me was because I'd fallen in love with Kurt.

At Brooker Hall, right away on that first day they had me signing in every 15 minutes. This was called "suicide checks". I thought they were crazy to think I was suicidal, for surely I wasn't in the least bit. I thought they were in this way trying to drive me crazy. I was very paranoid by this time and mistrusted everything and everyone.

Early on the second day in Brooker Hall, there was a group meeting. The meeting centered on a young woman by the name of Rachel who had just come to grips with the fact that she was an incest victim. It was the first time she had been able to face the fact that her father, a minister and a man she had loved and respected, was now the object of her horror. All throughout the meeting I couldn't help but think that she was me, even though there was never any incident like that in my life. She spoke of nightmares and screaming and pounding on the walls at night. The other patients were upset because she kept them awake.

I felt that I had the answer for her and wondered why no one had ever told her to "Just pound on your pillow. You can get all the anger and horror out that way without keeping anyone else awake." I was sure the staff wanted her to keep everyone awake in order to keep them sick. In fact, I felt that the staff had implanted that idea in her mind in order to make her sick and that nothing like incest had every really happened.

That evening after a lapse of time during which I was out of touch with reality altogether, I awoke to find myself strapped to a bed lying in my room. The windows were open and I was wet from urine. Because of the chill and the wet, I became so cold that my body shook violently. I heard shots and sirens and screams. I imagined that the window was open so that the police could aim at my head. I expected to be shot any second. I was so sure that death was near so I turned my head and read all the prayers that I had posted on my bulletin board. I read whatever prayers I could see by twisting my head as far as I could. I read them over and over. Then I resumed screaming.

Eventually someone heard me screaming, for they came down to my room, which was at the end of a very long hall, far beyond any other. They washed and dried me and wrapped me in warm blankets. Before I knew it they were putting me in an ambulance. When I asked, they said I had had an overdose of Thorazine. What they didn't add was that the overdose was due to the shots of Thorazine the doctor had given me earlier.

When I arrived at County Superior Hospital, they parked me on a cot in the hall. Two other patients were parked there also. I began to sing softly as I usually quieted myself in this way. I kept singing until they put me in a room and hooked me to an IV. I was so paranoid by that time that I had to read the list of ingredients which were in the IV before I'd agree to let them do it. The nurse put the needle in me and twisted it cruelly. Quickly a large bruise developed. When the doctor came I told him about what she had done. A little later I heard him scolding this nurse. I figured she probably thought I had attempted suicide. I reasoned that Dr. Steven probably never told them that he was the one who overdosed me.

After that I felt pretty good. I was back at Milwaukee Mercy the next day. The patients were all going on a field trip but I had to remain on the floor. I had the whole morning to myself so I settled in the community room. There were several shelves full of magazines. However, the magazines were put on the shelves with only the back seam showing. I couldn't tell anything about the magazines, looking at it arranged this way. So I made a project out of sorting all the magazines into piles and putting each stack of the same magazine side by side with the entire front cover showing. This made much more sense to me. Once again I concluded that the staff didn't want the patients to get interested in anything that would help them get better. They put the magazines on the shelves that way so that no one would read them. This only furthered my beliefs that they were trying to keep us sick.

That night, when the other patients had returned and we were all in the community room together, I noticed that almost all of the patients were playing games. To my great alarm and dismay, the games they were playing all had to do with psychology and psychiatry. My first and only reaction was that the staff planted these games in order to keep the patients sick. I myself was involved in something I felt to be very creative. I'd take a magazine and because we couldn't have scissors, I'd learned to fold and crease carefully, so carefully that it would look like I'd cut it with a scissors, and I'd choose meaningful words to cut out in this way. Afterwards I would arrange the words on a poster. To me this was very therapeutic.

The next day I noticed that every other patient had ordered snacks from the kitchen. I was convinced by this time that the staff, nurses, doctors, and counselors did everything they could to keep us sick and keep us patients. Having noticed that the snacks were usually sweets, milk, peanut butter and jelly sandwiches, I was sure that what my sister Janine had taught me probably applied, that the different foods were linked to mental illness by way of allergies. I was sure they were feeding all of the patients the exact foods they knew would make them sick or keep them sick. There was no way they could convince me to order a snack as I wandered aimlessly among all the other patients eating their way to illness. All the while I felt that I was a spy trying to uncover the many twisted methods used to keep Milwaukee Mercy booming.

One of the first days at Booker Hall, I noticed a very nice-looking older woman. Every day I noticed that she was wearing the same green dress. Once I happened to overhear one of the staff tell her, "You look lovely today in that pretty green dress. Is it new?" Later I went up to the woman and said "She's lying. You've been wearing that same green dress every day I've been here." After that I couldn't help but notice that the woman wore a different dress each day. In fact, I perceived how greatly improved she seemed to be. This only furthered my beliefs that they were trying to keep us sick.

I was told to try and get to know the other patients. In my mind one of the best ways I could think of was to lay out all my snapshots and label them. In the process, I was going to use the ping pong table to lay them on. I pulled out the ping pong table and it collapsed. Suddenly there were about five men right there at my side. They grabbed me and pulled me toward the quiet room. I figured that the reason they had previously made me sign in every 15 minutes was to make everyone think I was suicidal. Now that they were putting me in the quiet room, they were going to kill me and make it look like suicide. I pulled my earrings off and threw them and everything else that could be used as a weapon. I kept shouting, "I'm not going to kill myself." I didn't want anything they could later say I used as a weapon to kill myself. I was so sure that they were going to kill me that I wouldn't let them get near to give me a shot. They brought in a tray of medicine cups and tried to get me to drink all of them. I was positive that if I would have, there was enough there to kill me. I reached out and dumped the whole tray onto the floor. Later on they brought in a tray of food. I imagined they hid the medicine in the food, so I dumped that onto the floor as well, and refused to eat anything. I don't know why but I smeared the food around on the floor and before long the room smelled like a pigpen.

One of the reasons the quiet room smelled so bad was because when they first put me in there they said they didn't want to hear a sound. They were emphatic about that and I thought they meant they'd kill me if I made any noise at all. So when I had to pee, there was no alternative but to go on the floor. That, combined with the food smeared all over, made for a very foul-smelling room that was never once cleaned the whole time I was kept there.

I felt like I never slept, mainly because I was so frightened that they were going to kill me. But upon looking back I must have slept, for I was in there for three days and three nights.

If I folded my mat just right and stood on it, I could see out through a small slit above a painted window. Before going in to the quiet room I was carrying a bag filled with ideas for improving the hospital. I had quickly handed this bag to a man I'd seen standing around. I charged him with guarding my bag carefully until I came out. When I managed to peek out, I saw this man sitting outside the quiet room. I figured that he was guarding me so they wouldn't kill me.

For something to do, I decided to fold my mat as many different ways as possible. I was sure that I folded it 15 different ways. Now when I think about it, that would have been impossible. Besides singing and folding my mat, there wasn't much else to do. I can't remember most of the time I was in there. I would swear to it that I never slept a wink because of my fear of being killed. I also felt that they were trying to drive me crazy. They managed to give me a shot of Haldol and it made my thoughts turned upside down and backwards. I wouldn't let them get near me with the Haldol again.

Days of terror, nights of hell. I wouldn't allow anyone to come in alone, they had to come in pairs. My reasoning was that if one of them tried to kill me, the other one would be a witness. Towards the end I must have calmed down, for I walked around and sang every song I knew. I just sang and sang and sang. Perhaps this was what led to their letting me go. They couldn't take it any longer.

One day the nurses just came in and got me. They said that Dr. Steven said I could leave the hospital if I wrote a letter asking for release. I composed a three page letter. He then had me take a psychological exam, after which time he discharged me AMA, meaning Against Medical Advice. I learned later that my sister Janine had called and called. After not being able to contact me, she had pressured Dr. Steven into telling her where I was and then she had insisted on his discharging me.

Before I left, I had to go to the nurses' office for something. While I was there there was a telephone call for me and they put it through to me. Lee, a man I had known only a short time, called to say he would like to get together with me when I got out. I told him I was being discharged that very day. He told me he was sorry he couldn't pick me up but that he'd give me a call right away. He was the man who had just sold me a new car.

I can't remember much, but I do remember that first date with Lee. I dressed in a long-sleeved red nylon blouse and a black skirt with black heels. He was dressed like a real gentleman. He took me to a fancy restaurant with a piano player. He acted like he knew the piano player, as we sat right in front of him and they exchanged bits of conversation all night long. Afterwards Lee begged me to come to his place but I refused. He took me to Port Washington anyway, just so I could see where he lived. He made a very pointed effort to instruct me as to how to find his place.

Later at home, I realized I hadn't gotten a prescription filled for all of my medicine. It was too late to get it in West Bend so I had to drive to Milwaukee to get it. Just before I left for Milwaukee, Lee called. He made me think he was going to attempt suicide because I wouldn't go to bed with him. On the way to Milwaukee I thought of this conversation all the way. When I reached Walgreens, I asked the pharmacist what I should do. By this time, I had decided to go and rescue him.

I was all mixed up in directions, driving over 80 miles per hour, more desperate with each minute that passed. Instead of ending up in Port Washington, I ended up in Germantown, so I went to the police. The policeman told me to call Lee, which I did using their phone. When Lee understood what I had done, that I had contacted the police, he was furious. My mind was all mixed up about him.

PORT WASHINGTON, Wisconsin

"What is defeat? Nothing but education, nothing but the first step toward something better." Wendell Phillips.

The next day Lee called and we went out again. Only this time he convinced me that I should go to bed with him. He made me believe that that was the only way I could ever get well. I believed everything he said. Needless to say, he raped me.

Upon arriving at Lee's apartment, it oddly struck me that he was wearing a muscle shirt and was covered with tattoos. Up to that time, I had only seen him dressed up in a suit. It sent out a warning signal to me that this isn't the same man I knew.

The first thing Lee did was to go to his closet where he had stored boxes of poetry. He pulled down one box and shared some of his poetry with me. This gave me another warning signal. His poetry was filled with references to the devil and evil.

When he led me into his bedroom, I was struck by the beauty of it. A thought crossed my mind that t he must live in his bedroom. It's hard for me to believe that after all this, I would still crawl into bed with him. But I did. All throughout this ordeal my mind kept crying out, rape…he's raping me.

Afterwards, he took me out to the living room where he forced me to watch a pornographic video. At that time, I was wondering if he would let me go or if he would kill me. He let me go with the warning that I should go home and take a shower.

I didn't go home. I was too frightened. Instead, I went to the Holiday Inn and rented a room. From there I called my doctor and told him I had just experienced a date rape. He refused to see me. At the hotel I soaked in the bathtub for hours. Finally I felt brave enough to go home. But first I went to a hardware store and bought a very strong lock. When I arrived at my apartment, the first thing I did was to put this lock on my door.

One night shortly after I woke up and I thought I saw a man by my bedroom window. I called the police and they came and checked it out. They assured me that no one could possibly be by my bedroom window, as I was on the second floor and there was no door or porch near enough to the window.

Because of the trauma I was suffering, my counselor suggested that I go to group therapy. She mentioned a group that met at Martin Hospital. The group session was held at night. I parked in the dark parking lot and walked through the black, dark night to the hospital. Once I was in the hospital, I had to walk through some long, dark hallways to get to the meeting place. While walking, I was so fearful that I figured I'd never go again. During the group session, I listened to a young girl talk about incest. The entire meeting centered on her and her story. Needless to say, I never went back. I never received counseling for the rape.

It seemed that I would want Lee to be punished in some way for what he had done to me, but the term "willing rape" always held me back. In reality, there is no such thing as "willing rape". No one wills to be raped. And yet, I felt I was to blame. So I never went to Lees' employers and told them about it. To this day, I am sorry that I didn't, for I'm sure I paved the way for other women to fall into the same trap I had fallen into. It seemed so obvious to me that this was his way of life. I possibly could have put a stop to it if only I had spoken up. But I was too afraid. I was also too embarrassed.

The next morning I called Dr. Dick, a psychiatrist I had greatly trusted at one time. He invited me to come and talk with him, so I did.

That hour with Dr. Dick didn't help me at all. He insisted I tell him every last detail of the rape. I wasn't ready to talk about it, but he forced me to. Afterwards, I felt as though he had viciously torn me open and apart and I was very angry and upset. The next morning I called Dr. Dick and said, "Dr. Dick, you are both an extremely good psychiatrist and an extremely cruel one." He had given me a bottle of sleeping pills to help me through the crisis.

After making that call to Dr. Dick, I called Dr. Steven's office. When the receptionist answered, I said, "I have a bottle of sleeping pills in my hand which Dr. Dick gave me, and I'm about to swallow them." Believe it or not, she put me on hold. By the time she returned to the phone I had already swallowed the pills. When I told her this, she asked me for my address and said an ambulance would soon be there for me. I was still conscious when they arrived but slipped into unconsciousness before they got me to the door. They carried me out on a stretcher and took me to St. Joseph's Hospital in West Bend. I awoke the next day in the critical care unit with a big machine monitoring my heart. The remnants of the stomach pump were still down my nose but were soon removed.

Later in the day I met Dr. Matthew, who was my doctor while there. He talked to me in a very friendly and kind way. He said he realized that I was unhappy with the psychiatrists and told me he would like to help me. He was a general practitioner but insisted that he was very good with helping women and that a lot of women came to him for help. I just nodded and put it completely out of my mind.

While there, I felt totally miserable. The nurses were just as good to me as anyone could imagine. I couldn't understand why anyone would want to be nice to me. One evening I began to cry. Before long I was doubled up in pain, crying harder than I had ever cried in my life. The sobs just tore me apart. It was a long while before I could get any semblance of control. The nurses reflected my mood and were both compassionate and kind. One nurse cried with me. They must have found it hard to be around me because I was so sad.

Eventually they told me that I would be transferred to Wauwatosa Mercy Hospital. I told them about Dr. Steven and the quiet room and that there was no way I'd go back there. They insisted that I had to go. I decided that if I went back, I'd need some kind of assurance that I wouldn't be put in a quiet room and that if I were put into one, I'd ask for discharge and Dr. Steven would have to let me go.

There was a lot of rushing back and forth with messages, for I insisted that Dr. Steven had to tell the nurses themselves that he wouldn't put me in a quiet room and that if he did, I'd be able to leave the hospital. I finally left, very reluctantly and with great misgivings. I was once again on my way to Milwaukee Mercy Hospital by ambulance. It was already night when I arrived, so they put me right to bed. They had an aide sit next to my bed. Still, I just had to do it. I reached out and put my hand around the light bulb. Immediately, I was taken to the quiet room. Once there, I asked for paper and pen and wrote my request to be released. They had to call Dr. Steven, who immediately released me once again AMA.

It took the receptionist ages before she finally got a taxi driver for me. This was about 2 a.m. When I saw him come for me I was a little startled. But I wouldn't let myself be frightened although I wasn't looking forward to the long drive back to West Bend. We talked the entire way and he was just as nice as could be. I had to pay him $50 but felt it was well worth it. I even gave him a big tip. He carried all of my things to the door for me. I was home at last.

WEST BEND, Wisconsin

"When one is out of touch with oneself, one cannot touch others."
Anne Morrow Lindbergh

It was good to be home. Nothing ever lasted for me, not the good times, not the bad times. I was determined to start over and to get my life straightened out but I still had a drinking problem.

It was about that time that Dr. Matthew started visiting me. He told me that he was going to visit me often because I was so lonely. The second time he came, he asked me what day it was. He told me that it was Valentine's Day and that he wanted to give me a valentine kiss. I stood up waiting for him to plant a kiss on my cheek or forehead. Instead, he kissed my lips. I couldn't believe it.

I confided in a man friend about this doctor and he told me that a good way of getting rid of him would be to call his home. I called and his wife answered. It worked. I never saw him again.

I started dating an older man named Jim. One night Jim drove to West Bend from Stillwater where he lived. He wanted to take me to a church to hear a charismatic speaker. After we entered the church and heard the speaker for a few minutes, I became extremely agitated and ill at ease and decided to leave. I left without saying anything to Jim.

On the way home in my high heels, I became extremely dizzy. As

I went on down the street, weaving back and forth, I decided to stop in at the Alcohol and Drug Abuse Treatment Center which was only a block away. When I arrived, I had to go downstairs. Weaving crazily, I asked the lady for help. She immediately called an ambulance, so I ran out and tried to run away. Instead, the ambulance stopped and a couple of police cars stopped. They chased me and easily caught up with me. There were several people watching as they placed me in the ambulance. All I could think was, "Oh no, not again."

Upon reaching the hospital, a doctor examined me. He sent me home with the police accompanying me. He had found me extremely dizzy but felt that it was emotion related. After that I always asked for Dr. Luke whenever I needed a doctor, for I liked his tactful, gentle ways.

I experienced great difficulty sleeping at night during this period of time. Often I'd be up and walking the length of Main Street anywhere between 12 and 4 a.m. It was on one such night that I decided I needed to talk with Dr. Paul. I had never attempted to wake him up before, but this particular night I'd decided to pack my things into the car and leave for somewhere. In my mind there was only one person who could stop me, and that was Dr. Paul.

Dr. Paul was furious about being wakened simply because I wanted to talk. I made a few careless threats and said goodbye, but now he wanted to talk and insisted forcefully that I stay on the phone and keep talking. I have to mention that I hadn't been seeing Dr. Paul for very long before this and not only did I not know him well, but he did not know me well. He said that I should not hang up for any reason. We had a crazy intellectual conversation. He made me angrier by the minute and finally I told him that I was leaving to go on a long trip. I'm sure he didn't believe me, but the truth is, I did.

I packed my belongings into the car and drove off. Not knowing where I was going, I pulled off the freeway and drove into a little town where I felt safe and tried to get some sleep. But sleep wouldn't come. I took a few extra pills and walked to a nearby restaurant and bar.

SPRINGFIELD STATE HOSPITAL

"Challenges can be stepping stones or stumbling blocks. It's just a matter of how you view them." Anonymous

It has always been easy for me to strike up a conversation with people, friend and stranger alike, and before long everyone in the bar knew of my adventure. They were behind me all the way.

While there, I decided to call home to Hubertus and let the girls know where I was. To my dismay, when I told Anne Marie what I was doing, she burst into loud sobs. I had never heard her cry so hard. Ordinarily it would have been heart rending, but at this time I didn't have a heart and my adventure was more important to me than anything else in the world.

Once again I went to my car to try and sleep but had no success. By this time my body felt like it was immersed in pine cones. I felt awful. I took a few more pills. There wasn't much else I could accomplish in that little town so I drove on. Much later I stopped at the Holiday Inn and even though I didn't have any money I figured I could use my Visa card, aware the whole time that there was no credit left in my account. But I felt that if I could just lie on a bed perhaps I'd be able to fall asleep.

As soon as I hit the bed I decided to call Jake, the main contact for the National Alliance for the Mentally Ill. Jake had been helping me for quite some time. He was always very supportive, and I felt that I could tell him anything. When I called him and told him of my plight, he warned me that I was breaking the law by doing what I did. So I got up, dressed, made the bed and took my luggage downstairs to the main desk where I explained my situation. The man at the desk was very gracious, ripped up my charge slip and bade me have a good trip.

After this I was desperate for sleep. I tried taking more pills, but they didn't seem to help. My body tingled in a strange way. It didn't feel like a body anymore. I was extremely upset by the fact that I hadn't slept in two days, fearing for my mental health.

Then I thought of a solution. I was just outside of St. Louis, Mo. I stopped at a gas station and asked where I could go to have a drink. It was now about 1 a.m. The man showed me where to go. There was a bar back off the road about a mile away. He didn't tell me that it was a motorcyclist's hangout.

It felt strange to walk into that type of bar all alone so late at night. Anyone would have called me crazy for doing such a thing because the bar was back in the woods. Even after finding it, I wasn't sure it was a bar, as the outer appearance gave no sign of it. Evidently it was a camouflaged bar.

Having parked my car off to the side, I walked among all the motorcycles and entered sheepishly. At first everyone did their best to ignore me. I noticed immediately that I was the only woman in the bar. I sat at a table off and alone. Eventually a couple of young and very good-looking men walked over to me. They invited me to sit at the bar with them and proceeded to buy me drink after drink. I was talking pretty fluently, telling of my escapade, of my illness and of my attempt to fall asleep. I told them of the number of pills I'd taken before coming to the bar and mentioned that they had failed completely to relax me enough to sleep.

About halfway through the morning hours, they said I absolutely had to go with them to their house to sleep it off. I argued that I'd sleep in my car and was told that it wasn't safe. I didn't know how I was going to get out of this jam. I certainly didn't want to go with them to their house. Heaven only knows what they had in mind for me.

As things became more and more critical, I suddenly collapsed onto the floor. I could feel the men carrying me. They put me way off to the side on some chairs. I've never felt as I felt then. I knew I was dying, but I also knew that I was utterly incapable of crying out for help or of helping myself in any way. I could not speak a sound as I felt myself losing life itself.

Later on, after I had been unconscious for some time, the two young men came to take a look at me. They felt my pulse, which was almost nothing, and immediately carried me to their car and rushed me to the hospital. I knew nothing of this, but the bartender called me at the hospital the next day to see how I was doing and told me about all that had happened.

When I awakened the next morning, I had an IV in my arm. I was in a room with a little old lady who was at least 99-years-old. Being desperate for someone to talk with, I kept coaxing and coaxing and finally got her to say something. After some time passed, a doctor came to see me. "We almost lost you", were the words he spoke to me. He said they had contacted my ex-husband to tell him I was near death.

After an hour passed and no one else came along, I pulled out my IV and got dressed. I made a quick tour of the hospital and discovered to my dismay that I was in an Old Age Home. This really freaked me out, so I quickly found my way to the door and ran down the street. I walked to town but realized I had no idea where my car was or where I was, for that matter. So I walked back to the hospital and was greeted by a couple of men who were out to track me down.

They took me into an office where I was interviewed by a few expert looking professional people. They told me that they had decided to put me in Illinois State Mental Hospital, which was not too far away. On hearing this, I made several attempts to run away, but that only worsened my predicament. They gave me no choice, I had to go in the ambulance.

When I arrived at Illinois State Mental Hospital, I imagined that my reputation had arrived before me. They spoke of watching me carefully. They said I was uncanny in my methods of escape and resourceful in means of causing disturbances. They said I had a high IQ and that I wasn't to be trusted for a moment.

Eager to comply with this assessment, as soon as I entered I said I had to go to the bathroom. Once inside, I locked the door and they had no way of getting me out except to break down the door. I bargained with them. "I'll come out if you promise that no one will ever put me in a quiet room." They promised. I came out.

It seems to me that because I had lived for 20 years in a marriage where I was constantly treated as though I had no brains at all, I was bent on proving in any way possible that I was smart. I was quick to take advantage of every loophole, to assess every weakness, to grasp every opportunity to shine.

There was one big problem with this attitude. Being in the position I was in, a patient perceived as mentally ill, any action on my part, instead of seeming to arise out of intelligence, was assessed as belligerent and non-conformist and was quickly punished.

They had a place for me behind the desk and away from the other patients where an area was reserved for only the worst patients. It was a small area with two bedrooms without doors and a quiet room. Of course, the quiet room had one big locked door. During the day the patients sat out in the open area where my bed was, an area both dirty and uncomfortable. There were a couple of hard-back chairs, but most of the patients sat on the floor. Actually it was a very small area for the six of us. I strongly objected to being there but this only served to get me put into the quiet room—yes, the quiet room.

A patient by the name of Jane approached me and said, "If I attack you when you're sleeping, please don't hold it against me. You see, I'm violent and dangerous but I can't help it." A young woman named Nellie was sitting on the floor. She had the typical bangs cut straight across her forehead, hair straight and short, and she wore what looked like a gunnysack dress. She gave the appearance of not being too bright. It seemed as though she had hit upon a means of getting attention, for she sat there with her knees pulled up under her arms and kept repeating, "I'm going to commit suicide…I'm going to commit suicide." One of the nurses hollered at her, "That's not the way to get out of here." Later on I spent time tutoring her in the ways of getting out.

There was a young man sitting in a wheelchair who couldn't talk. He had been in a car accident and was missing a leg. They had diapers on him which were always saturated and caused the place to smell horrible. Sometimes when I would get beyond the point of tolerance, I would tell the nurse that he needed to be looked after. This only brought upon me their disgust and agitation.

There was a very old man by the name of Mike who never came out of his room. I could hear him shouting over and over, "I'm not going to bed. It's POISON. I'm not putting on my shoes. They're POISON". This poor old man was in a state of perpetual fear. It seemed to me that someone should try to help him get over his fears, but instead they only shouted at him.

My story is not about these people, it is about a patient named Meg. Meg was obviously very poor judging by her clothes and hair. She had on a sack dress and strands of straight hair fell over it in matted clumps. Her face was fat even though her body was not and she reminded me of an old rag doll someone had thrown away.

Often I would look up only to see Meg staring at me. As time went on, I saw that she wasn't really looking at me but she was looking at my dirty white tennis shoes. Then one day it seemed as though she summoned every ounce of courage and asked me about my shoes. She thought I must be rich to have such a beautiful pair of tennis shoes. She said she had never owned a pair of tennis shoes.

I realized that the other patients regarded me as a princess. Meg especially gave me that impression. She often engaged me in conversations about my shoes and told me of her lifelong wish to someday have a pair just like mine. So one day we traded shoes. She had on a pair of thick heels with open toes that looked like they had been made out of wood. How grand Meg must have felt proudly wearing the tennis shoes.

When the nurse spotted our shoes, she made us trade back again.

It was then that I told Meg about another pair I had at home and asked her if she'd want me to send them to her. Meg talked of nothing else. She asked me again and again, "Are you sure? You won't forget, will you?" I couldn't believe that a woman could become so fond of a simple thing like a pair of tennis shoes.

I remember how I used to sneak out of the area and take a shower. Some days I'd manage to get in two or three showers without being found out. But eventually my devious ways caught up with me and I was put in the quiet room. I'll never forget how the nurse's aide picked me up and carried me by grabbing my feet and arms. She pressed me tight against her steel key case which hurt me so bad that I screamed in pain. She was obviously doing it on purpose. Later on, when I had a chance to look at my leg, I found a huge bruise. I felt that it was totally uncalled for and only an indication of her anger and hatred. I guess it need not be said just why I so badly wanted to get out of there.

Yet something beautiful happened in that back area. It was Christmas time so one night I started singing Christmas carols softly and to my wonder, the other patients began singing with me one by one. Even the little old man who was so paranoid was singing. We sang, and to me it was our way of rising above the squalor and pain. Our singing was the most beautiful thing that could possibly come out of that place. It was a tribute to the fact that our humanness could rise above anything.

Something happened to me while I was at this hospital which I consider to be the most horrible experience I have ever had. It's very difficult for me to think about, much less write about, but I know that until I do it will haunt me. Perhaps if I can tell the story, I can "let go" of it and the memory will have no power over me any more.

I have no idea why, but one night a couple of male aides came and got me out of the quiet room where I was sleeping. They told me I was going to have to walk outside for a short time in order to get into another building. When we got outside, I easily slipped away from them and ran for all that I was worth until I realized that all I had on was light pajamas and a robe and that I had nowhere to go. It was a very cold winter evening. So I slowly walked back as they caught up to me. Because of this escapade, they felt I deserved the worst.

They took me into this building and put me into a different quiet room. It was a strange place. There was a small hall that was a centralized area. Behind each door was another quiet room. Once they put me in I never saw them again, that is until my unacceptable behavior demanded their presence.

Here too, I was trying to prove that I could outsmart their system. I tore the ties off of my nightgown and my robe and tied them all together. Then I put it around my neck and pounded on the door for someone to come and see. I guess what I had in mind was that I would look as though I were going to attempt suicide. What I was saying was, "You put me in here so I would have no chance of killing myself, but see…I thought of a way even in here." Actually, I had no intention of killing myself. I was just playing their game. Well, the game quickly came to an end because when they saw what I had done, they decided to put me in leather restraints.

This in itself wasn't so bad. I knew I deserved it. I had been in leather restraints often. But what I didn't guess was that they would stretch my arms up and out and my feet were pulled as far towards the bottom of the bed as possible. Initially it wasn't so bad. But staying in that fixed position for an hour makes one feel as though they're stretched out on a crucifix.

Time passed. Hour after hour passed and no one came to let me out or even to check on me. No one came that whole night to help me go to the bathroom. I just laid in it. As time went on, I became fearful that they had forgotten me and that no one would ever come. The pain was excruciating. I screamed and cried until there was no strength left in me to scream or cry. I didn't think I could bear the pain any longer. Think of yourself lifting a large package onto a shelf and how the muscles are pulled. Here the muscles were pulled like that, only there was nothing to alleviate them.

The night passed slowly, painfully slow. Finally morning came. I had been in leather restraints for seven hours. I started screaming once again and this time a woman came. I could hear her outside my door asking, "Has she been in there all night? Why hasn't anyone undone her?" Then to me, "You poor dear. We'll get you out just as soon as we possibly can." And so they did.

They moved me to another holding room where I was supposed to wait. While in that room I saw them bring a large, strong man into the central area. I heard them say, "He's supposed to be put in leathers, but there's no way I'm going to tackle him." Somehow that made me feel how unfair it had all been.

They took me back to the first building I had been in and I immediately went to the phone and called NAMI to tell them of my mistreatment. Before I knew it, they were preparing me for departure. Perhaps it was to my advantage that I had become such a problem to them. It probably speeded up my departure. Soon I was put in a wheelchair and into an ambulance. It was to travel over 200 miles, taking me back to my home state and my home hospital. What went with me were my memories—most of all the memory of Meg and my promise to send her a pair of tennis shoes.

On the way I tempted the two drivers. I offered to buy them a drink if we could only stop at a bar. One of the men was eager to do this, but the other man decided against it. I was planning on using my credit card to buy the drinks.

I never heard from Meg, but I had her address and the first thing I did on reaching home was to send her the tennis shoes. I can only imagine how lifted up she would be upon receiving them. I could picture her receiving the package and opening it with tears flowing down as she realized that someone, for once in her life, had thought of her and had kept their promise to her. Perhaps it made the rest of her life go a little smoother. Perhaps it made her feel more like the woman she wanted to be.

MENOMONEE FALLS, Wisconsin

"Kind words can be short and easy to speak but their echoes are truly endless." Mother Teresa

When I arrived at Community Memorial Hospital, I realized that I had a big job ahead of me of tracking down my car. From my hospital bed, I made several phone calls to the police. They told me that my car was parked at a gas station in the town. I have since forgotten the name of the town. Once I was discharged from the hospital, a friend drove me to Milwaukee to the Greyhound Bus Depot. From there I went to Streator, IL to my sister's house. My brother-in-law then drove me to that gas station to pick up my car which I drove back to West Bend.

I inherited, with all of this crazy, mixed-up life, an inability to sleep. One night I was feeling extra restless and ill, so I drove to the emergency entrance at Community Memorial Hospital and asked them if I could be admitted. I neglected to tell them that I had taken two sleeping pills. They didn't think I looked sick and turned me away. Five minutes later I fell asleep behind the wheel and crashed into a telephone pole.

I remember the crash vividly. For one thing, it woke me up. Somehow I could feel myself losing consciousness but kept fighting to stay awake until I would see someone coming. Minutes later I did see someone and immediately fell unconscious.

I woke up the next morning in the hospital with a heart monitor attached. My sternum was broken but there was nothing that could be done to help. It had to mend with time. It was close to my heart and that is the reason I was on the heart monitor.

It felt to me like I had been in that hospital 50 times at least. The nurses all knew me and were my friends. During that year, Dr. Paul developed a strategy with me. If he felt that I needed hospitalization, he also felt that I needed the least hospitalization possible. There were many times when he would put me in just for a day or two. There was a separate room for psychiatric patients right in the midst of the regular hospital. He would put me in this room and usually I would be fine after a couple of days.

CHICAGO, Illinois

"Remember happiness doesn't depend upon who you are or what you have; it depends solely upon what you think." Dale Carnegie

Chicago held a certain intrigue for me. Even while living in West Bend, I could not forget about Chicago. One afternoon I became anxious to go to the big city once more, so I boarded a bus and was on my way. On the bus I struck up a conversation with a man who sat behind me. When I talked about my illness, he told me he was a psychiatrist and proceeded to give me his card. I felt that he was lying and had made up fake cards. When we arrived at the bus depot, I had a hard time losing him.

Out on the street, I was heading for one of the tallest buildings I could see. I took the elevator to the top of the Holiday Inn and was pleasantly surprised to find myself entering a large hall with a floor show. A band was playing and a lovely lady was singing one of my favorite songs. I walked to the table nearest to the band. During the intermission, some of the band members came to my table and sat down and talked with me. Eventually, even the woman singer came over and talked with me. I continued to order drinks and sat there until the show was over.

In what seemed a short amount of time, they were ready to close. I discovered that I didn't have enough money to pay my bill and asked to write a check. They wouldn't accept a check because I was from another state and before long two policemen came over to my table. They discussed it among themselves and decided to take the cash I had and a check to pay the difference. The policemen then asked me where I planned to sleep that night and I told them I would sleep in the restroom. They said that I absolutely could not do that and proceeded to take me to a nearby hospital.

At the hospital, they contacted a psychologist who was to talk with me. While waiting for the psychologist, I was put in a room filled with beds and empty carts. I made myself at home and lay down on one of the cots until they came and got me. I spent the next four hours talking with first one psychologist and then another. Evidently the drinks had caused me to be very depressed and suicidal. By the time I was finished talking to the psychologists, it was morning and I no longer had to figure out how I would spend the night. Before letting me go, the psychologist had me sign a contract saying that I wouldn't try to kill myself.

I then took the "L" and went to St. Elizabeth Hospitality House. This was a new and very different experience. The House was filled with people in far worse condition than me. The thing that hit me the most was how dirty the house was. As I was shown different rooms, I completely lost it when I was shown the kitchen, as there were cockroaches climbing the walls. I slept in this house one night and then went to talk with the person in charge. I had to ask him for money to help me get back home. It occurred to me that he was either crazy, like the rest of us, or he was a saint. He lived in a big room with a board for his bed and a large crucifix on the wall. That was it. He talked with me a few minutes and then gave me money for the bus ride home. I was very anxious to leave that strange place.

WINNEBAGO, Wisconsin

"I expect to pass through life but once. If therefore, there be any kindness I can show, or any good thing I can do to any fellow being, let me do it now, and not defer or neglect it, as I shall not pass this way again." William Penn

On Dec. 29, 1988, I was taken to one of the worst hospitals in Wisconsin, meaning the hospital that took the worst patients. On the way, the policewoman warned me that if I ended up there too often, they would keep me there. I recognized the truth of that statement, knowing that patients were kept there for years at a time.

When I arrived, I was shown into a large room crowded with other patients. One patient stood out among the rest. He was all doubled up as if it were impossible for him to straighten out. His movements were jerky. I was revolted upon looking at him, thinking of him to be grotesque. His speech was unintelligible. I stayed as far away from him as possible, figuring that he was destroyed by drugs or that he was possessed by the devil.

That night I was put to bed in a room with another patient who fell sound asleep immediately. I couldn't sleep because of the noise right outside my door. When I opened the door. I saw the "creature" sitting on the floor just outside my door. Horrified, I slammed the door and hurried back to bed. But I couldn't sleep listening to the noises he made. I was petrified. I got out of bed and put my clothes on. After sitting on my bed for a time, I decided to go out and tell the nurse's aide to make the creature move away. It took every ounce of courage for me to open the door and address the nurse's aide nearby. He promised he would make the man move away, but five minutes later he was back by my door again.

I consider this to be the very worst thing to happen to me while in a mental hospital. I felt that the man was possessed by the devil and that the devil could easily come out of him and possess me. I was never so terrified in my entire life. All night long I sat on my bed fully dressed and ready to fight off any assailant, even the devil himself.

Morning finally came. With it, came the determination to leave this place as soon as I possibly could. I knew that meant that I must be on good behavior. That day I talked with a young girl. She told me her history that she had been a victim of incest. She wanted to die in the worst way. She finally told me that she had broken a spoon in half and had swallowed one part of it. I felt the need to tell the staff. Unfortunately, they had to operate on her.

The doctor in charge met with me in his office and reiterated what the policewoman had told me -— that this was my second time at that hospital. If I came back once more they would probably keep me there. By that time I was totally determined that I would never set foot in that hospital again. This was my last hospitalization before being introduced to Community Treatment Services and their program. Once I was in the hands of CTS, I became very involved in their outpatient program and began a remarkable recovery.

WEST BEND, Wisconsin

"Do not go where the path may lead, go instead where there is no path and leave a trail." Ralph Waldo Emerson

Eighteen years ago I chose to leave my husband. Because of the circumstances, I left my three daughters as well. At the time they were ages 15, 16, and 18. I decided to start over in a city where I knew no one in the city of West Bend. Here in West Bend, I've been able to put a broken life back together again, but in the beginning it was a very hard struggle.

It was in West Bend that I did my heaviest drinking. After my divorce, I lived alone for most of the time. When I would enter my apartment after a long day of work, I couldn't face the bare walls and would run out to the liquor store for alcoholic beverages. This became a pattern for me. At this time I was seeing a Division of Vocational Rehabilitation Counselor, Robert, and eventually he was able to confront me with my drinking problem. It was because of his advice and persuasion that I finally sought help from the Outpatient Program on Drug and Alcohol Abuse. I easily and readily absorbed the help that was offered to me, and continue to practice to this day the 12 Step Program which was introduced to me then.

After living in West Bend for four years and experiencing several hospitalizations during that time, I became a client of Community

Treatment Services, CTS, which was part of the Washington County Mental Health System. CTS is made up of a group of psychiatrists, psychologists, therapists, nurses and counselors who work together to help each individual mental health client. It is basically through CTS that I have been striving for the past 14 years to regain my health and to function once more as a citizen and member of the human race.

After an adult life ridden by breakdowns, starting when I was 21-years-old, I finally came upon people who understood me, understood my needs and offered the help necessary for recovery. I am now 63-years-old.

My life now flows evenly, easily and contentedly. This book is a look at the way my life was going, the way my life is now and a look into my dreams, hopes and goals. It has been said, "When God closes a door He opens a window". I can attest to that. Several windows have been opened for me. I want to share with you how this came about. It is a tribute to the programs I've been placed in, and more importantly, to the people behind the programs.

I want to thank the many people who helped me sometimes in ways against my own desires but always in ways devised with wisdom and insight, ways which eventually found me a willing client, as patients of CTS are called. I want to tell you of the many different people who have worked with me, both at CTS and IR (Industrial Resources). To my way of thinking, they formed a network of help that worked beyond imagining.

I changed so much that people who knew and loved me probably wouldn't even know me now had they known me when I was my sickest. God has graced me with many gifts. I say God has given, but it's implied in this statement that not only does God give, but also that I accept. He gives me the opportunity and I welcome it. Because of this, my life is now enriched with good health and many friends.

I simply refuse to submit to my illness. There is little time for me to sit back and feel sorry for myself or even to "experience" my illness. My entire being is consumed with the desire and the effort to overcome the limitations brought on by it. I am fiercely reluctant to attribute any shortcomings to my illness. My constant motto is "I shall overcome".

These thoughts are inherent in me, in my heart and in my soul. They are the air I breathe, a part of me that functions without any direction, without any planning and just as natural as drawing a breath. The only way I can explain this phenomenon is that the program here in West Bend worked for me. I didn't seek this program—I was directed to it. I did, however, seek the fulfillment of my dream to be well. It happened because of the caring and loving concern of the many people here in West Bend both on the scene and behind the scenes.

Behind every action, every word, even behind every thought, was this dream and hope that I could someday live a meaningful life— that this would be my future. I have chosen again and again to strive for a better life. I only hope that I am permitted to carry on the way I have been because what I'm doing is simply finding ways of being happy. This is because I've been led to live a meaningful life, and with this comes happiness.

One of the amazing things is that during some of my worst illnesses, I still managed to do some writing. My writing seems to be the one consistent element that brought sense to my existence. Without the opportunity to write, I may never have become well. I was a person with many feelings trapped within. Until I could find a conveyance for them, my thoughts and feelings stayed inside and festered. Once I discovered a way to express what was within me, I began healing slowly.

Here are the writings of a woman who has been diagnosed many times during the 40 years as schizo-affective and manic-depressive, a woman who has been on psychiatric medication for 40 years, one who has attempted suicide six times because of her illness and the hopelessness it caused.

This is my story, the story of a mental patient who struggles to make her life meaningful. I can honestly say I don't mind having a mental illness. I used to mind it so much I didn't want to live, but that time is in my past forever. I can see many things now that bring meaning and value to my life which I couldn't see before.

I live from minute to minute, discovering ways in which my life can bring meaning and color into the life of another, be it a fellow patient, a member of my family or a friend. Just by smiling, saying hi or making a friendly comment, I can make a difference in someone else's life. I don't need to be an important person like a doctor, teacher, or lawyer, but I can be important in my own eyes. That is really all that matters.

But, you might ask, what has wrought this tremendous change in you? I would answer in this way. I became a member of CTS, Community Treatment Services, at the Washington County Mental Health Center. I was given one-on-one counseling with such generous and dedicated people like Vicki, Karen, Kristine, Jennie and Bob. I became involved in Occupational Therapy and was shown love and attention by the encouraging words of Jamie and Tammy, the OT therapists.

I received medications carefully and lovingly from the nurse Diane. I was helped by numerous volunteers. I was made to feel important and wanted by Carolyn and Mary Lou, two of the finest receptionists in the world. I was treated as delicately and professionally as possible by the many different resident psychiatrists, the last one being Dr. Raja.

Then when I was ready, I was introduced back into the work world. At Industrial Resources I was taught how to do factory work and was smoothed into the areas of factory working. Then I took a step into the secretarial world by doing a clerical job at Threshold. All of this was done carefully, slowly and with much coaching and help. And consequently, all of it has been successful. I have every reason to believe there is no limit to what I can do in the future.

Up until now I haven't said anything about my spiritual life. About 14 years ago I started going to the Spirit and Fire Prayer Group. Here I was prayed over by loving and caring people. Those who prayed over me said that it would take a lot of prayer before I could be healed. It did take several years of prayer, but eventually I seemed to indeed be healed.

About six years ago, I became a member of a Catholic Lay Order. Under the careful guidance of a Spiritual Director, Father Matthew,

I received counseling of a spiritual nature. My previous moral upbringing flourished once again. I became a very honest and upright person as I had been prior to my days of mental illness. My spiritual life gave me insight and honesty. It provided me with inner strength and strong morals. Never again would I return to the days of my wayward past. Never again would I reject the path of righteousness that my parents had led me to respect. Never again would I turn to alcohol to solve my problems, or to men to find my answers.

The kind of life I am building today has something to do with every one of the people mentioned above. Each person plays a unique and vital part in my continuing recovery. As a result, I feel loved, cared for and important. These people form a patchwork quilt of love and caring. If one of these persons were missing, there would be a hole in my quilt. As it is, I can't say enough about these people and how important they are in my life.

And what is this life like? It is nothing important, but for me it is more than sufficient. I gain joy from little things, and there are many little things making my life so enjoyable. Most of these things are very simple and the joy I get from them is also simple, but it is enough for me and I guess that's what matters.

I love music. Music fills my soul with indescribable joy. Between my stereo, my boom box, and my radios I play all the records, tapes and CDs I can possibly handle. Country music, classical music, jazz and spiritual music are my favorite types of music.

I enjoy reading, listening to poetry being read, reading works of favorite authors and reading the news. My favorite is reading spiritual books. I feel life's ebb and flow through reading. It stimulates me to research and to write opinions, etc. Reading almost always leads me to write.

I enjoy writing. Writing is my vehicle for expressing who I am, what I am about and what my thoughts are on various subjects.

I love to learn. Often I study and learn new vocabulary words. Words are my passion. Whenever I meet a person who thinks like I do, dreams like I do and pursues similar avenues of learning, I go out of my way to become friends with that person. It is in this way that I discover good books, interesting classes and group activities.

When I have time, I love to paint and play the organ. I've recently started a scrap booking class, which will enable me to enhance all the abundant pictures of my grandchildren.

When I have an evening to myself, I light my candles, get comfortable and then delve into the many writings I have collected. Because I don't want to be distracted, I play my classical or spiritual music. Usually since I know how to get comfortable, I fall into a deep state of relaxation.

Each day I spend an hour of meditation getting to know my God. This is such an integral part of my day that I can't seem to function without it.

There's something very warm and comforting about waking up in the morning, stretching, yawning and realizing I've slept that night through and discovering that I'm thoroughly rested. At these times I lay in bed awhile and count my blessings. Then I get up and get ready for daily Mass. This is such a wonderful start to my day that I can't imagine my life without it.

For the last three and a half years I've worked in child care, taking care of my grandsons and granddaughters. When I arrive at my daughter Barbara's house, 4-year-old Adam races across the room with his arms wide open saying, "Gammy, Gammy!" He then runs into my arms as fast as he can. Jacob, who is 2 years old, jumps from his mother's arms into mine. No one could ask for a warmer welcome than I get from Adam and Jacob. Baby Lauren is now 5 months old. She smiles at me with recognition from across the room and I find that amazing.

As soon as I walk in the door at my daughter Kari's house, both of the 20 month old twins look at me with a big smile on their face. Even at that young age, Emma and Hayley know who their grandma is, and shower me with signs of affection.

I consider myself so fortunate that my daughters and sons-in-law trust me to take care of their babies. There was a time in my life when no one would have dreamed of trusting me with their babies. I feel that these experiences have contributed much to my present state of mental health. Nothing in this world is more beautiful and more helpless than a baby. When I am with them, I have no time to think of myself. I'm in an entirely different world when I'm with them. I become completely absorbed with their care and in return they give me their total love.

I'm also fortunate to have my daughter Anne Marie and her husband Joe as part of my family. Even though they live far away in Missouri, we keep in close touch with each other either by phone or through the mail. I am indeed blessed to have three daughters and three sons-in-law who love me dearly. I couldn't love them more if I tried.

A DAY ALONE

"Watch your thoughts; they become words.
Watch your words; they become actions.
Watch your actions; they become habits.
Watch your habits; they become character.
Watch your character; it becomes your destiny." Frank Outlaw

I had spent the entire year going in and out of hospitals. My counselor told me that I was an expert at knowing how to get hospitalized. He was right. If I wanted to be a patient on a mental ward, I simply had to act crazy, and that usually did it. But during my last hospitalization the doctor had told me I was not inpatient material. Outpatient, yes, but inpatient, no.

That left only one avenue of action open. I must learn how to manage outside a hospital as well as I had learned to manage inside one. My times of barricading doors shut, of running up and down the hall tearing apart all the decorations hanging from the ceiling, of entertaining the staff with new and creative methods of possible suicide that were all in the past. Now I had to learn how to function out in the world!

The very thought of it was frightening, but the reality of it was earth shattering! I remember it vividly—that Sunday when I had nowhere to go and no one to visit me would be a time when I would be by myself. How I remember the terror of it. But somehow I took hold of myself and said, "If this is what has to be, then I will do it." The important two words I will, motivated me to take a look at the situation. I was alone with myself for the first time in eons of months and days. That wasn't scary enough. I had no special thing to do, nothing pressing, nothing which had to be done. I was on my own.

I can't tell you how revolting that thought was. How was I to entertain myself? How was I to live with the empty shell I had become, the shell that shook in fear every time it looked at itself, the shell that was aware that it, I, was all by myself alone with my fears, my depressions, my anxieties and my obsessive thoughts? Surely they couldn't expect me to overcome all that, and by myself?

My negative thinking at that time could probably fill reams, but something turned it all around. I began to get thoughts like, if I was in the hospital, what would I be doing? My answer was that I would be doing "something". And so I thought of something to do which I really like to do. I liked doing crossword puzzles. My next question, I can't possibly be up and around? And so I dragged my mattress out to the living room floor so I could lie down all day if I chose. I did choose to lie down all day. Something inside of me protested that I was not well enough to be out of bed. Well then do it lying down, but do it - do something.

I gathered everything together and started out my day of working crossword puzzles. It was so interesting that the time passed rather swiftly. Before I knew it, it was dark out and I was hungry. So I made myself a meal. Afterwards when the dishes were done and I was again lying down, the thought struck me "Dianne, you did it. You passed a whole day by yourself." More thoughts followed, like, "If you can do it with one day, you can do it with two, and three and four." My future was beginning to look brighter already.

What shocked me most of all was that I had been interested in something. That small treasure in itself was a miracle. I didn't exactly look forward to a future of working crossword puzzles. I had solved a problem with more far-reaching results than that. I had solved the problem by thinking for myself. My thinking didn't have to stop here. There are many more interesting things to do in this world besides crossword puzzles. All I had to do was think of them. And it need not be said that I was on my way to health!

I can think of only one way to share with you how far I have come and why—by sharing some of my letters to Jennie, my counselor for the last 10 years, and Dr. Raja, my psychiatrist for the last seven years. I owe so much to both of these people that I am unable to express in words what they have done for me.

CORRESPONDENCE

Feb. 16, 1998

Dear Jennie, lately I feel as though I have been through a wringer. What else could possibly go wrong in my life? And yet, the worst reaction I had was to cry. I have gotten emotionally upset but haven't lost my mental health over anything. I don't know about you, but I'm proud of myself.

I have you and Father Matthew to support me in my emotional, mental and spiritual health. Both of you are very kind and understanding and supportive.

I won't make this much longer. I just want to thank you for being there for me when I needed you. Of course, I have the support of my girls. And yet, I hesitate to pour out my troubles on them because it affects them so. I feel that I can tell you anything and I have the trust that you will be strong for me. You have always proven this to be so.

I'm very grateful right now. This morning when I was so troubled, I sat down and prayed to God to help me. I guess above all I can trust in God to help me in my times of need. I am so fortunate to be in touch with my spirituality. Without it I would be lost. I must thank God over and over for helping me, and I must continue to trust Him with my whole heart.

July 27, 1998

Dear Jennie, since you assured me that it is all right to write a letter to you once in a while, I now assume that luxury.

When I talked with you, it sounded so ridiculous to say that I have an inferiority complex. The truth is, I was experiencing just that, but the truth is also that I should not experience it. I think if I were to make a rational choice, I could choose to think well of myself. Why I don't is a mystery. And yet, I do think I have control of my choices. I am trying hard to make a more rational choice. Whenever I find myself comparing myself unfavorably instead I say something of a positive nature to boost my self-esteem. It usually works and I don't find myself feeling so negative anymore.

I do believe that the reason I got into this mode of thinking is because of feeling mildly depressed. Everything in my life took on a negative aspect. Here at home I found it difficult to keep things clean and tidy. I definitely find it difficult to get motivated for such things as art work. I've decided to take the bull by the horns. The last two days I've done many jobs that have needed to be done for some time. Just doing that made me feel better about myself. I have an art project in mind that I plan to begin as soon as possible. Because I feel better about myself here at home, I'm motivated to try contributing to the conversation a little more frequently at work, even without feeling too self-conscious about what I say. And guess what? They respond just as naturally to me as they do to each other. No one seems to notice that it's difficult for me to talk.

In the long run, I have it very, very good. I always seem to manage to get out of my dilemma pretty much by myself. I think that happens once I recognize what my dilemma is, and I come to recognize that by talking with you. You are a wonderful therapist and conversationalist. I don't honestly know what I'd do without you.

When it comes to conversation, I usually don't have a problem at all, no matter how many people. It's only when I'm down on myself that I have a problem. Actually, I love to talk and am quite capable, especially one-on-one. If that weren't true, I wouldn't have the friends that I do have. I care about people and try hard never to offend anyone. I honestly don't think I could handle any more friends. I believe the secret of my conversation is that I'm a good listener. I don't interrupt people and if I agree, I do so heartily. I enjoy a good laugh. I do enjoy other's company.

Jan. 2, 1999

Dear Jennie, I feel I owe you an apology. My defiance in the face of your statements wasn't right. I was so determined to drink that I wasn't going to let anyone stop me. I haven't come to this point before—ever. I hope I never come to this point again. Little by little I am becoming convinced that to drink again would be a big mistake. I hope to stick with this conclusion. My hopes are to quit drinking altogether for the rest of my life.

I once again found an antidote for all of my troubles. Like years ago, I drank to drown out my sorrows. I've learned that alcoholism is a progressive disease. It starts where I left off 10 years ago, only now it has gotten worse over the years. That's most likely why I drank with such a vengeance. I can't understand why I would do anything so destructive to myself. I cannot comprehend why I would do that. I want to say to you "I'm sorry", but the real person I should apologize to is myself. I am sorry that I put you and myself through all of this.

Jan. 11, 1999

Dear Jennie, as for my drinking, that is in the past. I'm doing everything under my power to make sure it's in the past. I don't want that problem.

March 15, 2000

Dear Jennie, I love my new status as a member of the Catholic Lay Order. I love the prayer, the reading, the lectures and the Masses I go to almost daily. If this didn't make me different, then something would be wrong. If this didn't create in me a desire for poverty and humility and love, then I'd be misusing my station in life. I will say that it isn't all easy. There are many times when I'd like to skip my prayer, but most of the time, I don't, simply because I feel drawn to becoming the best Catholic I can be. I feel it is such a privilege. It is a part of my life where I don't carry any stigma as a mental patient. I'm just like all the rest. And I feel I can become a saint if I really want to bad enough.

Sept. 14, 2001

Dear Jennie, in a big way, this tragedy (the attack on America of 9-11-01) helped me come to my senses. I realized that the little pain I experience at work is absolutely nothing in comparison with the pain of others who were injured in the attack on America. I will venture to say that I was rescued by Adam (my grandson) from the fate of depression. Whenever watching TV got too much for me, I would turn it off and take Adam for a walk or just play with him. He never picked up on the somber mood but was just as happy as could be, all day, both days. He took peaceful naps and watching him was like a dream, seeing his peaceful little face in contrast to what I was watching on TV. On arriving home Wednesday night, I came to the conclusion immediately that he was the number one help to me over the past two days.

I can't believe the deep peace that is in my heart, in spite of the tragedies all around me. I have to believe that my spirituality is giving me strength...that and Zyprexa. I am so wholly and totally grateful to God for having brought me to such a state of well-being.

I shouldn't worry so much about when I can come and talk to you because I take the freedom of writing to you whenever I have a lot to say. Today at church, Father Matthew led Vespers Prayer Session. He is such a wonderful priest. I have been blessed many times in the past for all the Spiritual Directors I have had, among them Father Acquinas, Father Anthony and Father Luke. Father Francis was a close friend of our family for many years, until he died about three years ago. I have been near Priests for many years.

Today my heart is full, full of compassion for the victims and their families, full of compassion for the severe suffering which so many people are experiencing. But I found my soul's center at the Shrine Chapel. It seemed to me that Mary has her arms around our country. It seemed like Jesus, who suffered so much for our sake, now blesses the suffering of so many people. He blesses us with His mercy and His love. I feel strongly that every one of the victims is in God's hands dead or alive. As a nation, we are resolved to overcome and I, as one proud citizen, will overcome any evil inclinations in order to be happy and free.

May 27, 2001
Dear Dr. Raja, I am going to prepare you ahead of time for my next visit. I am very aware that I am much better these days than I have been for years. Due to lowered medication, I experience a whole new lease on life. I no longer shake all over, yawn continually and seldom lose my balance. My personality is much altered in that I don't have to ponder for a long time to come to a sensible conclusion. In other words, I'm much more alert and aware of what is going on around me.

This might prove to be enough for most people, but it is not enough for me. I sense that I have a long way to go before being the person I was years ago before my mental illness. Of course, I realize that I will never be the same as I was, but I believe I could come closer to that "me" of long ago. Now that I can taste the wonders of thinking and experiencing, I want to go back even further into the world of years ago. I do believe my medication prescription could be even less, and of course I will never know unless I try it.

That is why I'm writing to you—to ask you to lower my medication further than it already is. I would like to believe that you're a psychiatrist who believes in the least medication necessary for each patient. Of course there is a risk in lowering it, but I'm willing to take that risk. After lowering it if it proves to be impossible, I will be happy to go back on the 15 mgs. I know enough to know when I have failed and will certainly want to be at least as good as I am now.

Imagine if something happened to you to take away your thinking ability. Your entire life is dependent upon your mental ability. You would have to earn your living in an entirely different manner. Wouldn't you be extremely interested in any thing that could return your ability as it is now? That is what I'm asking for. Of course I will never be the same. I am sixty four years old, and was a lot sharper at twenty simply because of my age. But to me, sixty four is not very old. I should still possess my faculties intact at sixty four. I believe the medicine is what hampers my memory and my ability to think clearly. I admit that I could be wrong, but of course will never know unless I am allowed to experiment with my medication. This is asking a lot of you—to experiment with my medication. It may mean that you will have to see me more often for a short time. If this doesn't matter to you, it does not matter to me. I am willing to do whatever it takes.

P.S. Dr. Raja did lower my medication. I am now taking 12.5 mgs. of Zyprexa a day.

July 8, 2001

Dear Jennie, I tend to ask the question, "What is wrong with me?" That I am having so much trouble getting along with people. I tend to answer that question by saying that it isn't what I'm doing wrong but that I am so much more aware of what is going on around me. My tolerance level has dropped severely, to the point where I can't allow people to manipulate me any more. I must have been such a target for everyone before. I especially sense my mother trying to manipulate me and form my life and way of thinking. Of course, you must know me now and realize that I can't be manipulated any more. I think that this is a good thing, but I can't help wonder if it really is. Or am I becoming too proud? Why is it that I don't care to get along with these people any more?

I'm coming to you with the question, "Am I changing for the better or for the worse?" Is it better that I don't allow others to do my thinking for me—that I think for myself and end up disagreeing wholeheartedly most of the time? Is it better that I don't try to impress others with a me that isn't and instead let them see what I'm really like, what I'm really thinking? I have to tell you, this kind of mutating is very painful. I end up not knowing myself. Am I better off now than before? I have to think the answer is yes, because of the fact that I feel so much better.

April 17, 2003

Dear Jennie, this will probably be the last letter I'll ever write to you. I don't intend to bother you when you are in North Carolina. So I wish to write my last letter to you before you leave and before I meet with you for the last time. There are so many things I want to tell you and I think I can do it better in a letter than in person.

Where to start? How can I ever express the gratitude I have for all that you've done to help me over the years? There are no words. I wish to empty my heart of all its' emotion, and yet there are no words with which to speak. What you have done for me is beyond words. There is no telling of all the times you have helped me through crisis after crisis, no words to tell of the compassion and consideration you have always had for me, no words to tell of the sharing we've had with each other. I've always considered you as more than a counselor. You have been a true friend for me through all these years. This is the year for losing great friends. Remember, I lost my friend Laurie to a tragic automobile accident? Now I'm losing you.

But I don't for one moment feel sorry for myself. Just as I accepted the loss of Laurie because I know she has earned a better place, so I accept your loss because I know that you are listening to your inner soul. I know why you are leaving. I can understand probably more than anyone because I have my children near to me and they are my whole life. I am so fortunate to be able to watch my grandchildren grow up. Now you too, will have that option. I am totally happy for you. I seem to detect a spirit of adventure in you that I never knew you had. I respect you all the more for your decision which must have been a very hard one.

You have given me such support in the past. I don't know what I will do without that support, but having your support always made me stronger and I will use that strength to build a future without you.

I am so much stronger for having known you. I will never lose that.

I am so blessed with the spiritual life that I lead lately, knowing how helpful it is to building a stronger emotional life. I find that I possess such strength that I have never before realized. This is truly great! Because of this, I think people relate to me more deeply than ever before in my life. I think this is the reason I have so many friends. They see strength in me that I have never had before.

Once again I am reminded of how you have helped me zero in on all of my potential. I have such a wonderful life and I owe you many thanks for that. I always knew that I could turn to you. You were always there for me in my good times and in my bad. And because of this, my bad times have all but disappeared. I now know that there are answers for all of my questions, success for all of my quests.

I will always keep you in my thoughts and in my prayers. Thank you is not enough for me to say to you. I don't know how to thank you for all you have given me through the years. I have never, never been disappointed by you. You have always been there for me through the worst of times and through the best of times. I only wish I could express what I feel. I won't allow myself to cry over losing you because that would mean that I'm sad you're leaving, and I'm not sad. I'm thrilled that you have made this choice. I know that your life will be so much fuller when you have family nearby. I know from my own experience how much richer your life will be. I have no doubt that you will find a good job. I'll pray for that. I can't even imagine the wonderful things people will say about you in your job resume and opinions of the people who have worked with you and under you. They will all have the most wonderful recommendations for you. I have no doubt about that.

WHO IS MENTALLY HEALTHY?

Mental health, like physical health, is a dynamic, ever-changing condition. Some days you are bound to be in better shape than others. The mentally healthy person does not experience wide personality swings—on the moon one day and in the dumps the next. He/she has the qualities of sameness and predictability.

Mentally healthy people think well of themselves. They do not waste time and energy worrying if every hair is in place or if they made a favorable impression on Mr. X or if they used the right fork or wore the right dress. On occasion, when every hair is not in place or they may have used the wrong fork or worn the wrong dress they don't agonize over it. They have a good sense of priorities and know what is really important.

Mentally healthy people are able to accept whatever life visits upon them without going to pieces. This means financial reversals, illness, death, divorce, separation or unrequited love—the list is endless. And they have the ability to withstand the cruelties and inequities of life, to regroup, to re-energize and to think their way through a problem and go forward in a positive, constructive way.

When you are mentally healthy, you have interests, goals and dreams. You find that you are unable to sit by and watch life unravel. You absolutely have to be a partaker in life. You notice when life is unfair to others, you do your utmost to overcome this unfairness. If you see someone being discriminated against because they are different than others, you do what you can to deal out fairness and acceptance. Honesty and generosity become an innate part of you. If you find that you have spare time, you volunteer in one way or another. Your time may be your most valuable asset, and you use it generously.

Those who possess good mental health also possess kindness, firmness of purpose, generosity, fairness, determination and motivation. There isn't much time to sit around and feel sorry for yourself; because you believe time is of the essence. In other words, your time alone is valuable and your time to give to others is valuable. You make sure that you have both. Nothing seems impossible because your partner is God, who helps you do all things. A mentally healthy person has a deep faith in God and loves all people because they see God in each person.

CONCLUSION

WEST BEND, 2004

"Miracles happen to those who believe in them." Bernard Berenson

Now let me tell you about what my life is like today. My life is very full. It is full because I have so many commitments, I am close to my family and I have many friends.

Some of my commitments are an overflow of the great love I have for other people. I am involved in public speaking about my mental illness and mental health. Recently, I was elected to the Board of Directors for NAMI (National Alliance for the Mentally Ill) as secretary. I work at the Drop-in Center three times a month. While there, I talk with and try to help anyone who comes in seeking help or just friendship. I was asked to be the Program Director for the Drop-in Center but declined because of other commitments. I teach the first and second graders during Mass at my church, St. Frances Cabrini. Two days a week I help my daughter care for her year old twin daughters. I've also been helping my oldest daughter because she is expecting another baby. I help her take care of her two little boys. I attend a prayer meeting two nights each month. Also, two nights each month I volunteer at the Samaritan Nursing Home helping the elderly play cards. I belong to a Prayer Chain, which means I am asked to pray for people in need. I am a member of a Lay Catholic Order and act as secretary for the meetings. Being a member involves going to monthly meetings and living a prayerful life. Because of this, I have a spiritual director who gives me guidance in my spiritual life. I try to go to daily Mass. I also attend 12 step meetings once a week to help maintain my sobriety.

Many hobbies make my life complete. I play the organ, write poetry, do watercolor painting, do cross-stitching and I'm involved in a scrap booking club. I like to work out on my treadmill. At home I am surrounded with music. My favorite music is classical, but I also love spiritual, country, jazz and some popular music. To me, music is love in search of a word.

It seems as though I don't have much spare time, but I do save time to get together with my many friends. I treasure all of my friends because they touch my heart and make my life brighter and happier.

In my spare time I love to read and write. I correspond with many family members and friends. My reading is pretty much confined to reading spiritual books. I also listen to tapes of college lectures. These are made available to me by a very good friend.

I spend time each month with my counselor who is a psychologist. I see my psychiatrist every other month. They keep close tabs on me in order to guide me along a safe and healthy pathway. My psychiatrist prescribes medicine which I take faithfully because I know that it helps keep me well. Both of these men are an integral part of my life. I feel totally comfortable talking with them. For 10 years I had Jenny as a counselor and feel that I owe so much to her guidance, her kindness and her wisdom. Just recently she moved away, and I really do miss her. She was not only a counselor, she was a true friend. For all of these years I had no problem that I couldn't share with her and come back home with the answer.

For years now I have known a deep peace and great serenity. I must weigh everything in this light. If something takes away my peace and serenity, then it is not good. If something is right for me, then I will be able to maintain this peace and serenity. I will continue to be filled with joy. It is as simple as that.

God has been so good to me. These past few years He has lead me by the hand to a land that I never dreamed I'd be in. All of my past ills have disappeared. I am healthy once again. I give God all the credit. He has showered me with graces. These graces are what have brought me out of the land of pain and suffering into a land full of joy and happiness.

Printed in the United States
49852LVS00002B/385-390